A STUDY GUIDE TO

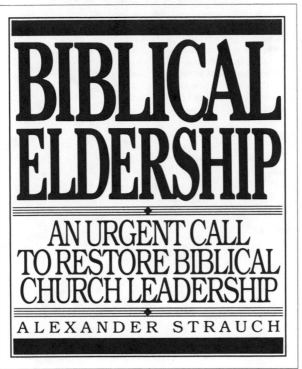

BIBLICAL ELDERSHIP

AN URGENT CALL TO RESTORE BIBLICAL CHURCH LEADERSHIP

ALEXANDER STRAUCH

LEWIS AND ROTH PUBLISHERS
Littleton, Colorado 80160 U.S.A.

Printed in the United States of America

ISBN 0-936083-01-8

Contents

Preface

A great, unperceived need among evangelical churches today is for a spiritual awakening to the doctrine and practice of biblical church eldership.

My justification for this sweeping assertion is that biblical eldership, more than any other form of church structure, best harmonizes with and promotes the true nature of the Christian assembly—particularly its family structure and humble, servant nature. Furthermore, although Scripture provides ample instruction and examples on this vital subject, it has been almost universally ignored by contemporary churches and teachers of the Word. Consequently, forms of church oversight exist that are totally unscriptural and detrimental to the spiritual maturity of the Body and true character of the Christian community.

I wrote *Biblical Eldership* as an expositional study book with the purpose of helping to restore church eldership to its rightful place. Further, I sought to expose false traditions that demean church eldership. Now I have prepared this study guide as a practical supplement to further reinforce the concepts presented in *Biblical Eldership.* Generally, this guide provides a format for church elders (or pastors and elders/deacons) to study what Scripture reveals about eldership and discuss the major ideas found in *Biblical Eldership* in a more practical way.

Since church elders form a corporate pastoral body, they need to study together, plan together, think together, decide together, and act together. In our Western culture— where extreme individualism and unbiblical ideas of freedom are prized—genuine, shared, brotherly leadership is difficult to envision. Moreover, because of our prideful, contentious flesh, it takes an enormous amount of effort and commitment for men to truly work together in harmony and humble, brotherly love. I hope this guide will help elders think and work together as a united, loving body of men. If they succeed, they will provide a dynamic example of true, Christ-like community to the local congregation and the watching world.

Specifically, this study guide has four purposes:

1) To equip men to defend and accurately articulate what biblical eldership is.

Most elders could not scripturally defend their belief in eldership if their lives depended on it. That is tragic, especially when we realize that the vast majority of Christian churches and leaders despise these precious truths. If we who believe in biblical eldership cannot defend it from God's all-sufficient Word, then we cannot expect others to hear or believe us.

Even worse, many who believe in elder rule do not clearly understand what it means. Lack of knowledge of scriptural truth is a source of endless problems and impoverishment among the Lord's people. As Hosea says, "My people are destroyed for lack of knowledge" (Hosea 4:6). So, a chief aim of this guide is to help men understand and defend what they believe about church oversight. In the words of the Proverbs, "There is gold, and an abundance of jewels; But the lips of knowledge are a more precious thing" (Proverbs 20:15).

2) To help elders evaluate their work and character.

It is imperative that church leaders regularly evaluate their work and character in light of the standards presented

2

in God's holy Word. It is all too common to find elders who think they are shepherding the flock when in fact they are doing nothing of the kind. Also, we all know how easy it is to lose sight of our priorities and duties, or misinterpret what Scripture requires of us. Evaluation is essential if we are to know where we stand before God, His Word, and our fellow brethren.

3) To motivate elders to improve their skills and effectiveness as a body of shepherds.

Every elder needs to improve the quality of his work, and every eldership needs to press on toward greater maturity. The problem is that few elders are concerned about taking specific steps toward improving their shepherding abilities or developing in spiritual maturity. Sloth, incompetence, ineffectiveness, apathy, ignorance, and mismanagement characterize too many elderships. Thus the Lord's people suffer from neglect and spiritual mismanagement. But there is always hope if the Lord is present. This practical guide attempts to motivate elders to think, pray, and talk about specific steps that will improve their skills and develop a spiritually mature, shepherding body.

4) To share practical suggestions and ideas.

Many elderships just need down-to-earth, practical advice and instruction. Of course, suggestions and ideas are only suggestions—not binding rules—and what works well in one church might fizzle in another. But one mark of an alive leadership body is *creativity.* There are countless ideas for improving in the areas of evangelism and shepherding, and one idea may produce other good ideas. Elders must be spiritually motivated and alert in order to use their God-given intelligence and skills for His glory.

If you have suggestions, criticisms, or ideas that might improve this guide, I encourage you to send them to me so that I can improve future editions.

A special word of thanks is due to John Denny, who worked through all the questions and made many helpful suggestions for improvement, and Barbara Peek for proof reading the final draft.

May the Lord give you greater love for one another, deeper insight into His precious Word, and fresh zeal and strength to serve His people more effectively.

Alexander Strauch
October, 1987

How to Use this Guide

I hope you will find the guide's questions, exhortations, and practical suggestions to be spiritually stimulating and helpful. Great care was taken to not create unnecessary controversy or personal offense. The guide is intended to build up the eldership, not tear it down.

Yet pain and effort are necessary to improve your eldership. Godly change is costly; sacrifice and discipline are necessary; correcting wrongs will hurt (2 Corinthians 7:8-11). Also, we are all easily threatened by evaluation and scrutiny. Our old ideas and habits die hard. Growth requires skill, hard work, and more time than we expect. So I encourage you to be patient with each other and pray. God's will is for you to grow in His grace and might.

The guide is divided into twelve group sessions. Before each group session, each elder should complete the lesson and be prepared to intelligently discuss the Word of God and the practical suggestions with the others. Do not wait until the night before a group session to do your lesson, because you will not have adequate time to read the assigned pages in B.E., memorize the verses, ponder the practical suggestions and exhortations, and answer the questions.

Each lesson takes from one and one half to three and one half hours for an individual to complete. If you complete one lesson a month, which I recommend, you will have a month to consider nine to twelve questions. If you work on three or four questions a week, you will not be rushed and will receive the greatest benefit from the guide.

Since many concepts of biblical eldership take time to fully grasp, do not rush through the questions and assignments in your group sessions. Although the guide has been designed to be done in twelve group sessions, many elderships should do less than one lesson at a time. It is not possible to predict how much time each lesson will take in group session, since each eldership's needs are different. It is even possible for an eldership to profitably discuss only two or three questions from each lesson if their time together is limited. The point is, do not hurry through the questions and suggestions.

The questions or assignments that require far greater time than allotted for your discussion sessions should be put off until later so that sufficient discussion and thought can take place. Record any question, assignment, or issue that demands further in-depth study or discussion on a "future discussion planning sheet." When you are finished with the study guide, prioritize the planning sheet and schedule times to study and discuss each topic.

All questions are to be discussed in group session unless otherwise stated. The practical suggestions, warnings, and exhortations should also be briefly discussed. Appoint a study leader for each session in order to control the discussion and keep the meeting on the right track. One controversial question could take the entire meeting time, so someone needs to guide the amount of time devoted to each question and suggestion.

Some questions will expose gaping inadequacies and needs in your eldership. You may at times feel overwhelmed by the task ahead of you, but do not let discouragement defeat you. Discouragement is one of the worst enemies of the soul. Ask God to help you be persistent in the face of problems and setbacks, remembering the words of our Lord that we "ought to pray and not to lose heart"

(Luke 18:1). It takes many years to develop a mature, good eldership, and you can only realistically deal with one or two major changes at a time. So be patient, but not passive.

Throughout the guide you will be asked to look up many Proverbs, so you may want to refer to commentaries on the book of Proverbs. (Charles Bridges' commentary on Proverbs is a devotional classic that should be on the bookshelf of every serious Bible student.) The reason for the abundant use of Proverbs is that elders are to be men of wisdom, counsel, and discernment (Job 12:20). Proverbs provides divine wisdom for all cultures and life situations. See Ecclesiastes 7:19; 9:15(a); Proverbs 21:22; 24:5,6.

All the questions and answers are based on the *New American Standard Bible.*

Although this guide is designed for group study, an individual can do the lessons alone and receive immense profit. Aspiring young leaders should be encouraged to go through the guide. It provides an excellent manual for training future elders. What an extraordinary blessing it would be for a younger man to have a church elder work through the guide with him. Also, all new elders should be urged to complete the guide.

Pray with me at this time that great prayer of King Solomon's: "So give Thy servant an understanding heart to judge Thy people to discern between good and evil. For who is able to judge this great people of Thine?" (1 Kings 3:9, cf 28).

A Plea

The once-a-month study sessions for B.E. take into account that the elders' shepherding work cannot stop in order to do these lessons. I encourage elders to meet weekly for three weeks to conduct their normal business and to study B.E. together on the fourth week. For elders who meet together only once a month, I urge you to prayerfully consider the following reasons for weekly meetings:

First, elders need sufficient time to pray. Christ is the Pastor, Head, and Overseer of the local congregation, and prayer is the primary way for the undershepherds to seek His guidance and will for the flock. Prayer, then, is a major responsibility of the church leadership body (Acts 6:4).

Furthermore, elders need to pray for the people: backsliders, broken marriages, weak and faltering saints, discord among the sheep, the unsaved, and *many private needs that cannot be publicly mentioned.* It is simply impossible to overstate the importance of prayer among the shepherds of the church. Our churches are involved in a horrendous spiritual battle. They are so vulnerable. Regardless of how big and successful your church may seem, there will be failure if the elders are not earnestly interceding in prayer for the flock. If elders meet infrequently, they have little time for earnest prayer amidst the normal business they must complete. Praying elders are watchful, alert shepherds. Never forget the words of Samuel to the people, "Moreover, as for me, far be it from me that I should sin against the Lord by ceasing to pray for you; but I will instruct you in the good and right way" (1 Samuel 12:23).

Second, elders need sufficient time to pray for one

another and to share their needs with one another. Praying for one another binds men together and greatly enhances interpersonal relationships, which builds a better team of shepherds.

Elders need to protect and care for one another because they are often under great pressure and spiritual conflict. They have weaknesses and faults that need the loving admonition of their colleagues. They have hurts and discouragements that need to be cared for (Proverbs 17:17; Galatians 6:2). The closer and friendlier the elders are to one another, the better they will handle the disagreements and frustrations that occur with one another. Also, the congregation will witness a better example of how all believers should live in brotherly accord.

To fulfill this important need, we begin our elders' meeting by having each man share his personal requests and concerns. This has helped us understand and care for each other better. If one of the elders is absent, we tape our meeting so he can listen to what was said. Let me also suggest singing together and sharing something to eat and drink; food and drink have a way of binding people together.

The following quotation by Robert Girard beautifully describes the ideal oneness and diversity of a Christian eldership that is functioning under Christ, the Chief Shepherd. I believe such glorious mutuality among men is not possible without meeting together at least once a week.

> But the New Testament does not teach that it is necessary or more desirable, for the effect of God's working, to place a single person in the "spokesman" or "bell sheep" role among the others equipped by gift and call to serve the flock as shepherds. In fact, it may be more in keeping with His design, to enable five men to func-

tion so totally as one, and to be so beautifully complementary to each other, and with such perfect diversity and equality of intensity, that neither they nor the church can see any clear distinction in terms of who is leading the leaders. They are "together." At one time, one seems to be leading. At still another time, the guidance, teaching, and nurturing seems to be flowing from the team, acting as one man. This phenomenon seems possible from New Testament descriptions of the life of some churches. It has the glorious potential of providing the church with a style of leadership that least obscures the headship of Christ.[1]

Third, the elders need to have sufficient, quality time to talk over the individual needs and problems of the saints. The elders' primary duty is to oversee and care for the spiritual concerns of people. This takes time. Elders need to inform one another about the needs and problems of the saints. *Good communication among overseers* is absolutely essential for effective shepherding care. All elders need to hear reports by their fellow elders of visits, phone calls, and certain counseling situations so the whole body can fulfill its shepherding responsibilities.

An effective eldership will have key people in the church who occasionally meet with the elders for discussion and decision making, i.e., Sunday school superintendent, youth leaders, Bible study leaders, returning missionaries, heads of important committees. In certain situations a person or couple may also need to meet with the whole eldership (B.E. pages 141,142). Multitudes of problems and miscommunication can be prevented when the elders meet with the people on occasion. Moreover, when people meet with the elders, the close, family character of the church is enhanced.

11

Fourth, situations and questions arise that require the elders to search out the Word of God for counsel and for discerning God's mind. This takes time in addition to all else that needs to be done.

Fifth, elderships that meet monthly often do not work as a team. Instead, one or two men do most of the work independently and report to the others at the monthly meeting. This practice fosters one of the most damaging notions about church eldership—that elders are the official, legal, church board, not the shepherds/overseers of God's people. This concept makes elders executives instead of pastors of the flock. Sheep don't need executives; they need loving, skillful shepherds who labor in the fields beside them.

Never underestimate the significance of your elders' meetings. Your meetings should be a time of rich blessing, during which you refine character, sharpen your skills, train younger elders, seek God, deepen in wisdom, and enjoy happy fellowship. I believe the Spirit of God works in special ways when men unite to seek His guidance and help. Such meetings produce greater care and blessing for the whole assembly. Bruce Stabbert personally expresses the exciting privilege and blessing of shared, brotherly leadership and the necessity of meeting weekly with fellow workers to pray and care for the Lord's household:

> They [the elders] are responsible for guiding the church people by making wise decisions and by careful administration. To do this, they must be humble men of prayer. They must be conscious of sound principles of management and decision-making. They must not be impulsive or dictatorial, but rather cautious and concerned for the feelings of the church. This requires that the elders meet together at least weekly, in order

to pray together and superintend church life. Our elders meet on Monday nights from seven to eleven or twelve. These times have been some of the greatest hours in my life, to sit among Spirit-filled men who are humbly seeking Christ's direction for the church. There is every prospect that men of diverse perspectives will be able to lead together with a blessed unity, if they submit themselves one to the other in the fear of Christ (Ephesians 5:21).[2]

NOTES: 1. Robert C. Girard, *Brethren, Hang Together* (Grand Rapids: Zondervan Publishing House, 1979), pages 243,244.
2. Bruce Stabbert, *The Team Concept* (Tacoma: Hegg Bros. Printing, 1982), page 167.

SESSION ONE

OLD TESTAMENT ELDERS AND ACTS 11:30 (B.E. pages 137-155)

Begin Your Session by Reading This Passage:

And in the proportion that any of the disciples had means, each of them determined to send a contribution for the relief of the brethren living in Judea.

And this they did, sending it in charge of Barnabas and Saul to the elders.

ACTS 11:29,30

Scripture Memory Assignment:
Acts 20:33-35.

1. a. In brief, point fashion, list the responsibilities of the elders of Israel (B.E. pages 141,142,150,151).

b. Although today's elders do not offer sacrifices, protect manslayers, or sit at the city gate, there are fundamental similarities between the responsibilities of the Old and New Testament elders. List three or four of these similarities.

c. As you surveyed the duties of the Old Testament elders, which of the duties that you discovered have sharpened your understanding of your responsibilities as an elder?

15

2. What highly significant lesson for elders do you find in Joshua 24:31?

3. a. By and large, Israel's elders failed to do their job: to uphold the law of God and protect the people. What were some of the root sins and failures of Israel's elders (B.E. pages 143-147)?

   b. Can you identify any of their bad tendencies in your own life? (This question is not meant for group interaction.)

4. a. Job was a model elder and details some of the things he did for people as a community leader in Job 4:3,4; 29:12-17,21; 30:25. Read these passages and list Job's activities or character traits as a community leader.

   b. What inadequacies in your personal ministry does Job's example expose? Discuss these together.

5. Job complained that his friends, who may also have been elders, were miserable comforters: "'You are all worthless physicians,' 'Sorry comforters are you all'" (Job 13:4; 16:2). Many elders today think and act like Job's friends. What characteristics do you observe in Job's friends that you as a servant of God's people should avoid? Look up Job 12:5; 13:4; 16:1-4; 17:10; 19:2,3,5,21,28; 26:2-4.

Practical Exhortation:

   In the Bible, the elders are referred to as the "elders of the people" or "elders of the congregation." *Eldership, then, is a people-oriented job.* It is teaching people, leading and guiding people, protecting people, admonishing people, visiting the sick, caring for the needy, and seeking those who stray. Eldership is shepherding people.

   In many churches, however, the elders are simply church board members, decision makers, or executives.

They are not shepherds of people who care for a family of brothers and sisters. The elders are uninvolved in the lives of the people, and the people don't go to them for guidance or help. In such churches the communal life of the church has given way to the institutional.

If you are an elder, remember that your work is caring for people, for an extended family—the household of God. Therefore, see that you are *not sidetracked or neglectful of your primary duty of watching over the souls of the Lord's people* (Hebrews 13:17).

Let me assure you that you will have to reevaluate this issue many times in the course of your ministry as a busy church leader. Indeed, you may want to do this right now.

6. a. In light of the last two questions and practical exhortation, explain how Matthew 25:34-40 could revolutionize your thinking and work with people.

b. Take time now, as a group, to pray and ask your heavenly Father to give you a genuine, caring heart for His people. Pray also that your eldership will be protected from being neglectful of its primary responsibility to shepherd the flock of God.

7. a. The first time Luke mentions the Jewish Christian elders is in Acts 11:27-30, when they receive a love offering for the poor saints. From the following verses, list the attitudes, thoughts, or actions that should characterize Christian elders (and all Christians) in regard to the poor and needy. Deuteronomy 15:7-10; Psalm 41:1; Proverbs 14:21,31; 19:17; 21:13; 22:9; 29:7; 31:8,9,20; Acts 4:34,35; 20:34,35; 2 Corinthians 9:7-9; Galatians 2:10; James 2:15-17; 1 John 3:16,17.

b. When elders exemplify lives of sacrificial concern for the needy and poor (Acts 20:35), what great biblical truths does the congregation learn? List only three or four.

c. How can loving, Christian care for the needy affect your congregation's evangelistic efforts?

8. List specific things that you and the congregation are doing, or could do, to express Christ's wonderful, sacrificial love for the needy and the poor. (Here is a situation in which the deacons and the congregation can help you. Don't forget to use them! See Acts 6:1-4.)

SESSION TWO

ACTS 15:1-29; 14:23; 20:28
(B.E. pages 155-174)

Begin Your Session by Reading This Passage:

And the apostles and the elders came together to look into this matter.

ACTS 15:6

And now the following day Paul went in with us to James, and all the elders were present.

ACTS 21:18

And when they had appointed elders for them in every church, having prayed with fasting, they commended them to the Lord in whom they had believed.

ACTS 14:23

"Be on guard for yourselves and for all the flock, among which the Holy Spirit has made you overseers, to shepherd the church of God which He purchased with His own blood."

ACTS 20:28

Scripture Memory Assignment:
    Acts 14:23; 20:28.

1. a. Acts 15 is an important example of how church leaders and congregation met together to resolve internal, doctrinal confusion (verses 4,5,7,12,22). List at least two situations that would require the elders and congregation to meet for discussion or dialogue.

b. Discuss the practical suggestions below and how you might implement them.

Practical Suggestions:

1) Since the local Christian assembly is to be a close-knit family of brothers and sisters in Christ, elders must guard against acting as an aloof, ruling oligarchy.

Hence, free and open communication must exist between elders and congregation. Christian elders must fully innoculate themselves against aloofness, secrecy, or independently seeking their own direction. The vibrant health of the eldership lies in its keen hearing, sensitivity to fellow brethren, flexibility, and desire to involve every part of the body in the process of living in harmony together (B.E. page 30).

2) The elders need to hear from the people they lead. They need the counsel of their brethren. It is a common fallacy for elders to think they know what the congregation thinks and needs; time and again I have been helped by hearing the insights and complaints of some of my fellow believers during joint elder-congregation meetings. Motivated by fear, some elders avoid all such confrontations, which greatly frustrates other thinking, caring believers. (Read B.E. pages 363,364).

3) The elders and congregation need to meet together occasionally for discussion and consultation. (Corporation laws may require a meeting of all members.) It is good for a church and its leaders to meet at least once

---

a year to go over budgetary proposals; to discuss any doctrinal shifts, program, or personnel changes; to talk about future plans; or identify weaknesses or problems that need attention.

4) It is also advisable for elders to meet with special groups within the congregation for discussion and counsel. For example, the parents of teenage youth might need to meet with the elders to air complaints or suggest solutions concerning youth programs. (This is a common issue for many churches.)

Ignoring issues or problems solves nothing, yet this is one of the most common failures of leadership. We must understand that loving confrontation is part of the job description for all elders or leaders. Although such meetings can be very trying, open communication eases many conflicts and erases most complaints. By not meeting with the whole church body or groups within the body, the elders hinder a vital part of real life together in the body.

5) The elders need to view public meetings as vitally important teaching times. During these meetings, the shepherds model how a Christian is to handle disagreements and problems. They model self-control, forbearance, love, and many other Christ-like qualities that should mark the Christian life. The best sermons ever preached on brotherly love, humility, and servanthood are not preached from the pulpit, but from real-life, everyday situations.

6) As overseers and leaders of the congregation, the elders should oversee or chair all such meetings. The meetings should be conducted in an orderly manner, with ample time given to open discussion or presentations

regarding new proposals from members of the congregation. If you read the Acts 15 passage carefully, you will find guidance for your own situation, especially if it involves doctrinal conflict. The apostles and elders were certainly not fearful of open dissent or dispute (verses 5,7).

2. Do not be surprised by doctrinal controversy. The first Christians had serious, fundamental debates over doctrine. Even the apostles' presence did not stop disagreement. As illustrated in Acts 15, it is the elders' responsibility to deal with doctrinal controversy. They must hear opposing views, weigh arguments, arbitrate between people, keep control of potentially explosive situations, and be able to fairly articulate the issues. What qualifications listed in 1 Timothy 3 and Titus 1 equip elders to resolve doctrinal differences in a thoroughly Christian manner?

3. a. Elders are often caught in the middle of difficult and perplexing situations. No matter what they decide will result in disagreement and unhappiness from some individual or group within the church. What is your opinion about the counsel that the elders and James gave Paul in Acts 21:20-25?
　　b. In threatening situations like the one confronting the elders and James at Jerusalem, fear is always a major motivating force. Fear of what others will think or do paralyzes many leaders from doing what is best or making necessary changes. From each of the following Scripture texts, make brief observations about the danger of fearing man's reactions: (Genesis 26:6-11; Exodus 32:21-25; 1 Samuel 15:24; Proverbs 29:25; John 12:42; 19:12,13; Galatians 2:11-14).
　　c. Can you identify any crucial issues or decisions that you, as an eldership, are avoiding, or scriptural truth you

are disobeying, because you are afraid people will leave the church or criticize you?

Practical Suggestion:
Many Christian organizations and churches have been seriously crippled because their leaders were afraid to confront troublesome issues or people. Be assured that if you confront problems, you will be criticized and face troubles. But if you don't confront problem issues, you will also be criticized and will have far greater problems in the end. You cannot run away from problems without causing more serious problems. So you need continual courage, strength, and wisdom from God in order to face life's many battles and problems. Pray daily that God will deliver you from the fear of man and give you courage and strength.

---

4. List three reasons why Acts 14:23 is such a pivotal text to the doctrine of eldership.

5. Certain denominations and scholars teach that Paul and Barnabas merely presided over the church's election of its elders. Carefully study note eleven (B.E. pages 187,188). In your own words, summarize the points made in this passage for rejecting congregational election. Discuss these points together so that everyone clearly understands them.

6. a. In short, Paul's final message to the Ephesian elders is to guard the church from false teachers (wolves). Since guarding the church from wolves is a major duty of the eldership (B.E. pages 112-115), list three essential qualities a shepherd must possess before he can and will effectively guard (protect) the flock from dangerous wolves or other predators.

b. In specific terms, what must an eldership do to guard or watch over a congregation of God's people? The following verses give examples of the different aspects of guarding the church: Acts 15:1,2; Galatians 2:11-13; Philippians 3:1,18; Acts 20:31; 1 Timothy 4:11-13; 2 John 10,11; 2 Timothy 2:16,23.

c. What qualifications in Titus 1 and 1 Timothy 3 go along with this aspect of the shepherding task?

7. a. Carefully read the quotation by Richard Baxter from his book *Reformed Pastor* (B.E. pages 170,171). Do you believe "the enemy has a special eye on you"? In what ways?

b. As shepherds of the church, elders have great influence over the flock. If you, as an elder, cannot guard your commitment to the Gospel or spiritual walk before the Lord, how can you protect the flock? The truth is, you may well be responsible for leading the church astray, which many church leaders have done over the centuries. Do not overlook the close connection between the person and his work, the teacher and his teaching (1 Timothy 4:16).

What are you presently doing in the way of personal spiritual disciplines to guard yourself against falling prey to doctrinal error, spiritual defeat, or satanic traps? Write down what you actually do and how much time you devote to doing it. This assignment is to be done privately. (Note carefully 1 Timothy 4:6-16; 6:20,21; 1 Thessalonians 5:17; Revelation 2:2-5; Luke 10:38-42.)

8. a. The church eldership is not another committee or organizational board. It is a body of Spirit-placed men appointed to oversee the church (Acts 20:28). This is an effective form of leadership and protection for the church.

How do you know the Holy Spirit placed you in the church as an overseer?

b. How should knowing that the Holy Spirit, Himself, sovereignly placed you in the church as an overseer affect your shepherding work? List at least two ways it should impact your work and thinking.

9. The Holy Spirit has placed the elders as overseers to shepherd the local flock of God. However, the impact of the shepherd imagery is lost to most modern people. Let's study Palestinian shepherding so we can fully understand and utilize this beautiful image. Look up the following references and describe in your own words what the work of shepherding entails.

These questions are to be answered privately, not in group session. The verses are grouped in general categories to make the study easier for you. Be sure to look up all the verses. B.E. pages 107-117 will also be a helpful resource here.

a. Which aspect of the shepherding task is set forth in these verses? 1 Samuel 17:34,35; Isaiah 31:4; John 10:11-13; Ezekiel 34:8(a); Amos 3:12.

Personally evaluate yourself in this area of shepherding. Write down the two numbers that best represent your performance.

9	8	7	6	5	4	3	2	1
Strong point		Good		Average		Poor		Sheep in Trouble

What practical steps can you take to improve your performance? Think in terms of concrete ideas and things to do, such as making one phone call a day or one home visit a week.

b. What aspect of shepherding is set forth in these verses?

25

Numbers 27:17; 2 Samuel 5:2; 1 Chronicles 17:6; Psalm 78:70-72; 80:1; Isaiah 40:11(b).

Personally evaluate yourself in this area of the shepherding task. Write down the two numbers that best represent your performance.

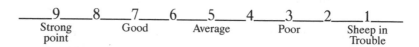

___9___8___7___6___5___4___3___2___1___
Strong   Good   Average   Poor   Sheep in
point   Trouble

What practical steps can you take to improve your performance?

c. What aspect of the shepherding task is set forth in Jeremiah 3:15; Ezekiel 34:2,8(c),23; Revelation 7:17?

Personally evaluate yourself in this area of shepherding. Write down the two numbers that best represent your performance.

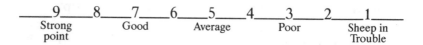

___9___8___7___6___5___4___3___2___1___
Strong   Good   Average   Poor   Sheep in
point   Trouble

What practical steps can you take to improve your performance?

d. What aspect of the shepherding task is set forth in these verses: Ezekiel 34:6,16(a); Jeremiah 23:4?

Personally evaluate yourself in this area of shepherding. Write down the two numbers that best represent your performance.

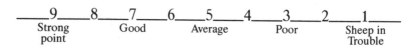

___9___8___7___6___5___4___3___2___1___
Strong   Good   Average   Poor   Sheep in
point   Trouble

What practical steps can you take to improve your performance in this area of work?

26

e. What aspect of the shepherding task is set forth in Psalm 28:9; Isaiah 40:11? (You do not need to evaluate your performance here or in the two following points, unless you choose to do so.)

f. What aspect of the shepherding task is set forth in Luke 2:8; Jeremiah 31:10; 33:13?

g. What aspect of the shepherding task is set forth in these verses: Isaiah 13:20; Jeremiah 23:4; 33:12; Ezekiel 34:15; Psalm 23:2?

Practical Suggestions:

1) I recommend that you read Phillip Keller's books, *A Shepherd Looks at Psalm 23* and *A Shepherd Looks at The Good Shepherd and His Sheep*. I have read both books several times and they have greatly enhanced my awareness of sheep and the shepherding task.

2) If you travel anywhere in the world where there are shepherds, even if they are not in the Near East, do all you can to talk to them about sheep and their work as shepherds. This will help you understand the biblical image of the shepherd and his sheep.

---

10. In Acts 20:17-28, the terms *elders, overseers* (bishops), and *shepherd* (pastor) all appear together. In your own words, explain the significance of this fact in light of traditional church practices.

Practical Exhortation:

Almost all false teaching is bolstered by changing the meaning of words. As lovers of Scripture, you must become acutely aware of the word game. You must discipline your mind to discriminate between how biblical terms are commonly used today and how they were orig-

---

inally used.

This is especially true of the word *pastor* (we will look at the term *bishop* later). The word *pastor* conveys concepts to the average person that are completely foreign to the New Testament. I know of no way to solve this problem except by dropping the word *pastor* and using the term *shepherd*. I use the word *pastor* in this book simply to jolt your thinking and help you realize that, from the New Testament's perspective, elders pastor the church. The word *shepherd* does not carry the unscriptural connotations that the term *pastor* does, so it is a more neutral term. It is essential that you clearly understand how the verb and noun forms of *shepherd* are used in the Greek New Testament in connection with Christian leaders.

The verb *shepherd* is used three times in the context of Christian leaders. Our Lord ordered Peter to "shepherd My sheep" (John 21:16). The elders' duty is to shepherd the church, and twice they are reminded to shepherd the flock of God (Acts 20:28; 1 Peter 5:2). The noun *shepherd* is only used once to describe Christian leaders, and that is in reference to spiritual gifts (Ephesians 4:11).

There are only two offices described in the New Testament: elder and deacon. There is no office of shepherd, just as there is no office of teacher or evangelist. Not confusing office with spiritual gift, we can say that some elders will have the gift of shepherding, but that all gifted shepherds will not necessarily be elders, e.g., itinerant shepherds. In summary, the eldership is the official shepherding body of the local church, and some of the elders will have the spiritual gift of shepherd.

SESSION THREE

ACTS 20:28-38
(B.E. pages 174-185)

Begin Your Session by Reading This Passage:

"Be on guard for yourselves and for all the flock, among which the Holy Spirit has made you overseers, to shepherd the church of God which He purchased with His own blood.

"I know that after my departure savage wolves will come in among you, not sparing the flock; and from among your own selves men will arise, speaking perverse things, to draw away the disciples after them.

"Therefore be on the alert, remembering that night and day for a period of three years I did not cease to admonish each one with tears.

"And now I commend you to God and to the word of His grace, which is able to build you up and to give you the inheritance among all those who are sanctified.

"I have coveted no one's silver or gold or clothes.

"You yourselves know that these hands ministered to my own needs and to the men who were with me.

"In everything I showed you that by working hard in this manner you must help the weak and remember the

*words of the Lord Jesus, that He Himself said, 'It is more
blessed to give than to receive.'"
And when he had said these things, he knelt down
and prayed with them all. And they began to weep aloud
and embraced Paul, and repeatedly kissed him, grieving
especially over the word which he had spoken, that
they should see his face no more. And they were
accompanying him to the ship.*

ACTS 20:28-38

Scripture Memory Assignment:
Acts 20:29-32.

I encourage you to also memorize verses 17-27 and 36-38; it is not that difficult. You could write each verse on a card and memorize one verse a day while you drive back and forth to work. In a very short time these wonderful words will be inscribed on your mind and heart, ready to use as you daily labor for Him. Don't forget to refresh your memory of these verses every so often!

1. a. Discouragement is one of the most prevalent problems elders face. It is a chief reason why many leave the work. Discouragement is also the source of many bad decisions and wrong attitudes (Genesis 42:36; Numbers 11:10-15; 1 Samuel 27:1; 1 Kings 19:1-4,10). Problems and situations arise that cause every elder to think, *Is it worth all the frustration?* When you experience discouragement because of those you care for, remember Paul's words to the elders in the latter part of Acts 20:28, and ask yourself these questions:

(1) To Whom does this congregation belong?

(2) At what cost was this body of people obtained?

(3) How does God feel about these people?

30

(4) How do I need to change in order to see the congregation the way God does?

b. After answering these questions, do you sense what a tremendous honor it is to be an elder? Do you realize what a serious matter it is to neglect the care of the church of God? Look up the following verses that show the immense value of the Church in God's eyes. In a short paragraph, state how these verses should affect your thinking and work as a shepherd of His flock. (John 10:14-17, 27-29; 17:6; Romans 5:8; 8:31-39; Ephesians 1:22,23; 2:19,22; 5:25,27; Colossians 3:12(a); 1 Corinthians 3:16,17; 2 Corinthians 6:16; 1 Thessalonians 1:4; 1 Peter 2:5,9,10.)

c. At this time, pray that God will give you a heart like His for His church, no matter how small or problematic it may be. Only then can you be steadfast in the face of many weaknesses, failures, and discouragements.

d. Sing together "The Church's One Foundation." It will challenge you to the task of guarding the local church of God which the Spirit of God has given to you.

The church's one foundation Is Jesus Christ her Lord; She is His new creation By water and the Word: From heav'n He came and sought her To be His holy bride; With His own blood He bought her, And for her life He died.

Elect from every nation, Yet one o'er all the earth; Her charter of salvation—One Lord, one faith, one birth; One holy name she blesses, Partakes one holy food; And to one hope she presses, With ev'ry grace endued.

'Mid toil and tribulation, And tumults of her war, She waits the consummation Of peace for ever more; Till with the vision glorious Her longing eyes are blest, And the great church victorious, Shall be the church

31

at rest.

2. a. Since false teachers are likened to wolves, you need to know something about the temperament, habits, and traits of the wolf. Using whatever resources you choose, write a short character description of the wolf.

b. The elders have been given the mandate to guard the flock of God from wolves—that is, false teachers. Thus, shepherds must know as much as possible about the character of their arch-enemy, the false teacher. Using the following groups of verses, list and discuss the chief characteristics of the false teacher as outlined in Scripture.

(1) 1 John 2:26; 2 John 7; 2 Corinthians 11:13; 2 Timothy 3:13; Titus 1:10.

(2) 1 John 2:22; Revelation 2:2; 1 Timothy 4:2.

(3) 1 Timothy 6:5(b); Titus 1:11; 2 Peter 2:3,14; Jude 16.

(4) 2 Peter 2:10-12; 1 John 4:6; Jude 8-10.

(5) 1 Timothy 6:4(b); Titus 3:9.

(6) Romans 16:18(b).

(7) 1 Timothy 6:4(a); 2 Peter 2:18; Colossians 2:18(c).

(8) Deuteronomy 13:1-5.

(9) Jude 19(c).

Practical Suggestion:

It is important that you, as a protector of the flock, be able to defend the truth from predators. At some point in your ministry you need to study the cults, false religions, or false representations of biblical Christianity that operate in your locality. It is not enough to simply study beliefs; you must understand how false teachers reason and think, particularly how they twist the meanings of words and biblical concepts. You must also under-stand their mind set and training.

---

3. The most frightening warning given to the elders is found in Acts 20:30, "and from among your own selves men will arise, speaking perverse things, to draw away the disciples after them." Do you see that the Spirit of God has given you the responsibility and authority to guard the local church from perverse teaching of the Gospel? If so, then write out some specific steps you as a body of elders would take if someone from within the congregation were to arise and begin teaching perverse doctrine in order to draw "the disciples after them." For additional help refer to Acts 15:1-29; Titus; Galatians 2; Jude; Revelation 2:2.

4. a. Devout people in the congregation (including the elders) who deeply love God's Word will inevitably have legitimate disagreements over the interpretation of certain Scriptures or doctrinal issues. This may cause some contention. What is the difference between godly people who disagree and the people Paul warns against in verse 30?

b. If you don't clearly understand this distinction, you may wind up falsely accusing your brethren, who love the Lord, of evil—just as you would pernicious false teachers. This problem has divided many good churches and many good brethren. List at least two distinctions between false teachers, referred to in verse 30, and holy brethren who honestly see things differently. To a great measure, the answer is found in the verse.

Practical Warning:
    I do not desire to hurt or offend anyone, but a warning is in order for those who continue to divide and pick apart the household of God over doctrinal differences. Some people have rigid, narrow, hypercritical dispositions, and are suspicious of anyone who is different. A hypercritical spirit is judgmental of almost everyone

---

and tags anyone who disagrees—even in the slightest way—as liberal, false, or compromising. The terrible tragedy is that people of such dispositions tear apart godly people who love the Lord and His Word. They divide people who otherwise have 95 percent agreement on all major doctrine. The hypercritical, narrow-minded person will always find something to pick at and separate from. He or she may seem very spiritual and right, but the action is just another expression of the flesh; it is religious pride. The spirit of the Pharisee must be turned away from and confessed as sin.

One qualification for an elder in God's household is *forbearance,* a beautiful word meaning gracious, conciliatory, and gentle. A forbearing spirit shows "a willingness to yield and patiently makes allowances for the weakness and ignorance of the fallen human condition" (B.E. pages 228).

If you want to understand forbearance or graciousness, study how Paul handled disagreement and differences among the saints. To the Philippians Paul said, "Let your forbearing spirit be known to all men . . ." (Philippians 4:5). He himself was a large-hearted man, always trying to accentuate the positive and make peace among brethren. His tolerance for differences, his flexibility, his commitment to unity, and his patience in handling serious doctrinal problems is a rebuke to us all (Acts 21:21-26; Romans 14:1-15:13; 1 Corinthians 9:19-23; Philippians 1:15-18; 2 Timothy 2:24-26; 4:2). If we were more like Paul, we would not have the thousands of church splits that exist today. Let us hold firmly to our doctrines, but in the proper, forbearing, Christian spirit (2 Timothy 2:24-26; Ephesians 4:15).

5.   Upon Paul's departure, he left the elders of the church in the care of God and His Word (verse 32). It was the elders' task to trust in God and His Word so that they might be built up for the fierce battles that were to come. Are you conscious of the fundamental need to trust God more in your trials and to seek His Word continually for wisdom and strength? Explain how the following verses illustrate the truths set forth in Acts 20:32: Deuteronomy 17:18-20; Joshua 1:8; Ezra 7:10; Job 23:12; 2 Chronicles 14:9-12; 20:20; Psalm 44:6,7; 62:8; Proverbs 3:5,6; 16:20; Daniel 3:28; 2 Corinthians 1:8-10.

Practical Suggestion:
   When facing critical times, decisions, or problems, prayer accompanied by fasting is an appropriate expression of total dependence on God for guidance, deliverance, or help. (See Ezra 8:21-23; Matthew 6:17; 17:21; Acts 13:2,3; 14:23.)

---

6.   What significant lessons are revealed by Paul's example of earning his own living while evangelizing and shepherding the churches? The following verses will give you some help: 2 Thessalonians 3:7-11; 1 Corinthians 9:14-19; 2 Corinthians 11:12,30.

7. a. Note that Paul envisions that those who oversee and shepherd (pastor) the church earn their own bread. But this is an unacceptable practice to many Christian people today. Why do you think people resist the concept of church shepherds earning their own living, or tentmaking?

   b. Neither God's Spirit nor Paul, the great church planter, would have established an ineffective or harmful form of church oversight. What does the fact that the first churches were shepherded (pastored) by ordinary men who earned their own bread by tentmaking reveal about the nature of the church? Read B.E. pages 94-105.

8. Read the following quotation by R. Paul Stevens about tentmaking elders. Discuss together its validity and your reaction to his suggestions:

> And for tentmakers to survive three full-time jobs (work, family and ministry), they must also adopt a sacrificial lifestyle. Tentmakers must live a pruned life and literally find leisure and rest in the rhythm of serving Christ (Mat. 11:28). They must be willing to forego a measure of career achievement and private leisure for the privilege of gaining the prize (Phil. 3:14).
>
> Many would like to be tentmakers if they could be wealthy and live a leisurely and cultured lifestyle. But the truth is that a significant ministry in the church and the community can come only by sacrifice (*Liberating the Laity,* Downers Grove: Inter Varsity Press, 1985, page 147).

9. a. What two vitally practical life principles do you learn from Paul's example (Acts 20:35) that you as elders should earnestly seek to emulate?

b. What does God's Word assert about these two life issues? Look up all the Scriptures cited and summarize what God says.

(1) Leviticus 19:10; Job 30:25; 31:16,19; Psalm 72:13(a); Proverbs 17:5(a); 19:17; 29:7; Ezekiel 16:49.

(2) Proverbs 6:6-11; 10:26; 15:19; 20:4; 21:25; 24:30-34; 26:13-16.

Practical Exhortation:
If you are employed, God's will is for you to give your employer a full, honest day's work. A conscientious, hard-working employee is a sterling credit to the Gospel and the local church. If you are slothful and only like to do "spiritual" work, then you have much to learn about spirituality and the Gospel. You will be a disgrace to the Lord's people and the gospel message.

c. Read together and briefly comment on the following verses as they relate to you as elders: Ephesians 6:5-9; 1 Timothy 3:7; Titus 2:9,10; 1 Peter 2:18-20.

SESSION FOUR

FIRST THESSALONIANS 5:12,13
(B.E. pages 191-201)

Begin Your Session by Reading This Passage:

But we request of you, brethren, that you appreciate those who diligently labor among you, and have charge over you in the Lord and give you instruction, and that you esteem them very highly in love because of their work. Live in peace with one another.

1 THESSALONIANS 5:12,13

Scripture Memory Assignment:
1 Thessalonians 5:12.

1. a. Some scholars contend that Paul did not appoint elders for his newly planted churches because he did not directly address the elders in his letters to these churches. How would you answer this charge?

b. In your own words explain why Paul, in his letters to the churches, did not call on the elders (or any other leaders) to handle problems or difficulties within the church?

c. As elders, how do these facts affect your thinking toward the congregation and your work?

2. a. Critics say biblical eldership doesn't work because a board cannot properly care for a church. To these critics I heartily answer, "Amen!" Most organizational boards (church boards, too) are quite passive, uninformed, and uninvolved, but biblical eldership is something quite different. First Thessalonians 5:12, like Acts 20:28, shows what makes biblical eldership an exceptionally effective shepherding body for the church. The key is found in the Greek word *kopiao*. What does *kopiao* mean?

b. Look both at the meaning of *kopiao* and particularly its plural form. How do its meaning and plural form demonstrate that biblical eldership is an exceptionally effective form of pastoral care?

c. Look up the following verses, and in your own words show how each verse applies to the Lord's work or 1 Thessalonians 5:12. Proverbs 10:4,5; 12:24; 14:4; 14:23; 18:9; 19:15(a); 22:13; Ecclesiastes 10:17,18; Nehemiah 4:6; Jeremiah 48:10(a); Matthew 25:25-28.

Practical Exhortation:

God made man to rule, to be creative, to work, and to be productive (Genesis 1:26-30; 2:15), but sin has robbed man of his full potential. One evidence of this is that man in his fallen condition is plagued by laziness. Laziness is a worldwide social problem. Spiritual laziness is an enormous problem in the Christian church. The Proverbs give numerous warnings about the awful consequences of laziness.

Because most elders have three jobs—the care of the church, their family, and tentmaking—it is important to clearly understand what God says in His Word about the value of work. In our pleasure-crazed world where people are preoccupied with self, a biblical work ethic is unwelcome, as are the principles of self-denial, self-

---

discipline, and sacrificial living. Yet these principles are undeniably an essential part of a busy elder's life. That is why this study includes so many verses pertaining to the work ethic. As an elder you will never be able to shepherd the church, care for your family, and attend to your employment unless you are willing to work hard, discipline your life, and even deny yourself certain legitimate pleasures and activities.

Of course the work ethic can be pushed to harmful extremes. Work can become an all-consuming idol. It is wise to remember that our Lord—a diligent, hard worker Himself—was concerned about rest for His disciples. He was not a harsh and unsympathetic Master (Mark 6:30-32; Matthew 11:28-30; cf. 2 Chronicles 12:8).

Paul Stevens provides an insightful solution for hard-working elders. He insists that tentmaking elders find their rest and contentment within the very rhythm of their life's work—as they move from tentmaking, to home care, to shepherding the larger family of the local church. He suggests that the change of spheres of service helps prevent burn out, which would occur from doing too much of the same thing. Tentmaking elders are also in a better position to understand others within the church because they, too, share the time pressures of tentmaking, family responsibilities, and maintaining personal spiritual vitality, as well as carrying heavy responsibilities within the Christian community. (*Liberating the Laity,* pages 143,144.)

Balance is absolutely essential to the spiritual and domestic health of an elder's life. Sin creates imbalances that are destructive to families, churches, and individuals. So every elder should seek to live a balanced, Christian life through the help of the Spirit of God, family, and friends.

3. For biblical eldership to operate properly, the elders must be willing to make personal sacrifices. What do the following verses teach about self-sacrifice: 1 Chronicles 21:24; Malachi 1:14; Mark 12:41-44; Romans 12:1,2; 2 Timothy 2:3,4; Acts 20:24?

4. If an elder is to properly care for his family, nurture the church family, and earn a living, he must be disciplined. What do the following verses teach about self-discipline: Galatians 5:22,23; Titus 1:8; 1 Corinthians 9:24-27; Proverbs 25:28; 16:32?

5. a. For an accurate understanding of your responsibilities as an elder, it is essential to understand the meaning of the Greek term *prohistemi.* In your own words, write a simple definition.

b. List some English synonyms of *prohistemi.*

c. Where else in the New Testament does this term appear? Does that passage(s) have special relevance to our study? In what ways?

d. To be effective, elders must have a clear understanding of their identity and function in the body. How does the term *prohistemi* help you better understand your place and work in the local church?

6. a. For an accurate picture of your task as an elder, you must also understand the meaning of the Greek term *noutheteo.* Describe what *noutheteo* entails.

b. List specific situations or problems that would require you to admonish your fellow believers.

c. How would you admonish a fellow believer?

d. Why is admonishment an important responsibility of the elders?

7. a. In light of the strenuous work of the sacrificial elders at Thessalonica, who led and admonished the congregation, how should the saints respond to the elders (B.E. page 130)?

b. What reason does the inspired writer give for the congregation's obligation to highly esteem its elders? (Read and briefly discuss together B.E. pages 98,99.)

Practical Suggestion:

First Thessalonians 5:12,13 exhorts believers to know and esteem their dedicated leaders. By nature, however, people are ungrateful and forgetful. Please read the following passages of Scripture: Genesis 40:23; Judges 8:35; Esther 6:2,3; 2 Chronicles 24:22; 32:24,25; Job 19:14,19; Ecclesiastes 9:15; Luke 17:12-18.

One of the most pleasant, dedicated, Christian couples I know poured their lives out for their church for 35 years. At one time or another they served in every major department of the church. But when they retired and moved away, they received not one card or word of public thanks for their years of service. Only after they were gone did people realize what had happened, so there was a feeble attempt to express some thanks. What an appalling illustration of the ungratefulness of the human heart!

As a church leader, you can set an example of a thankful, appreciative spirit (Romans 16:3,4). Cards, public acknowledgments, and dinners are a few of the ways to express appreciation and should be a part of your work. Others in the assembly can help in this effort by organizing and watching for opportunities to show appreciation. When you're busy it's easy to miss someone; call on others to help you with these details.

It's impossible to encourage or thank people enough.

So be liberal with your words of appreciation. Hardworking Sunday school teachers, youth workers, deacons, and many others need your words of thanks. Just a little word of gratitude will go a long way in encouraging and uplifting these people. If you're the type of person who finds it difficult to verbally express your love and appreciation, then ask the Lord for help. He can help you improve this dimension of your life—for the sake of the congregation as well as for your family's welfare. (See Proverbs 27:5.)

8.   Read very carefully our Lord's parable of the pounds in Luke 19:13,15-26 and list the significant truths from the passage that should influence your thinking about your work as a servant of God.

SESSION FIVE

FIRST THESSALONIANS 5:12,13
(B.E. pages 200-203)

Begin Your Session by Reading This Passage:

But we request of you, brethren, that you appreciate those who diligently labor among you, and have charge over you in the Lord and give you instruction, and that you esteem them very highly in love because of their work. Live in peace with one another.

1 THESSALONIANS 5:12,13

Scripture Memory Assignment:
1 Thessalonians 5:13.

1. a. To whom is the statement, "Live in peace with one another," addressed?

b. From the two lists of elders' qualifications (1 Timothy 3; Titus 1), list six that require elders to be peaceful men. Read together Proverbs 26:21. If you desire, commit this verse to memory.

Practical Exhortation:
As a body of elders, you need to regularly pray for the peace of your assembly. In all your decisions and

45

discussions, the peace of the congregation should weigh heavily on your judgment. But as much as God desires that His people live in peace, elders can never permit peace at any price (see Acts 15:1,2; Galatians 2:11-21).

2. a. Among the qualifications you have just listed, one stands out above all others for preserving peace when you face disagreement and failure. Using pages 227 and 228 of B.E., define in depth the meaning of this wonderful quality of character and how it can preserve peace among the Lord's people.

   b. Explain how the following verses illustrate this qualification: 2 Corinthians 10:1; 2 Chronicles 19:1-3; 30:17-20.

3. a. If you have read missionary biographies or talked to church workers who serve around the world, you will know that interpersonal conflict among Christians is at the top of their list of problems. Fighting among people is the scourge of the sinful human race. So do not be shocked or dismayed when you see fighting among believers. If you understand that fighting is part of human nature and that God uses these unpleasant struggles to test, expose the heart (1 Corinthians 11:19), and develop love, humility, and the servant spirit within His people, you can have the right mental attitude toward conflict among believers. Read and discuss together Paul Billheimer's excellent quotation on love and conflict within the local church, B.E. pages 131,132. (Also read B.E. pages 12,13.)

   b. Read Psalm 133 and explain how verse two can be applied to the elders, and consequently to the unity of the church.

   c. Read together Proverbs 6:16,19(b); 20:3. Discuss how these verses affect your thinking about God and your ministry.

46

4. a. Read Proverbs 18:19; 17:14; 19:11. Write out a brief, simple explanation of these verses and how they apply to you as elders.

b. Read together Proverbs 15:1. As a leader among God's people, you should memorize this verse. It will save you many sorrows, unpleasant apologies, and unnecessary conflict.

5. a. Using the following verses, list the key attitudes and actions that ruin the peace of the eldership and the church.

(1) Proverbs 13:10; Galatians 5:26(a); 1 Corinthians 4:6,7,18

(2) Proverbs 15:18; 14:17(a),29(b); 29:22; 30:33; Genesis 4:5,6,8

(3) James 4:11,12; Matthew 7:1-5; Romans 14:3,4,10,13; 1 Corinthians 4:5

(4) Proverbs 27:4; James 3:14,16; 1 Corinthians 3:1-3; Acts 7:9; 2 Corinthians 12:20

(5) James 4:1-4; Philippians 2:3,4

(6) Proverbs 18:6,21; 11:9(a); James 3:2,6,8,9

(7) Proverbs 26:20

(8) Matthew 18:35; 2 Corinthians 2:6-11

b. List two sinful attitudes from the list above that you struggle with the most. Spend time praying and asking your heavenly Father to help you gain victory over these sins so that you may not cause conflict or ill feeling among your fellow believers. This is to be done privately.

c. List two sinful attitudes from the list above that your assembly is most prone to exhibit. Together discuss how you would admonish the assembly regarding these sins.

Practical Suggestion:

At our annual meeting of the church corporation, our elders end the meeting by setting before the congregation a fresh vision and challenge for the new year.

This often includes exhortation on a particular weakness or failure of the assembly. Along with this exhortation, we present ideas and proposals for solving the problem. A leadership body that cannot regularly articulate to the group its failures and progress is a very ineffective leadership body.

6. a. Christianity provides lofty principles to enable God's people to live in unity in the midst of a divided and hateful world. If the church elders do not exhibit these principles of Christian living in their struggles and disagreements with one another and other saints, they will never be the role models God intends them to be, nor will they experience unity and peace among themselves.

Look up the following verses and discuss principles or virtues that should govern Christian behavior and attitudes. Remember, knowing these truths is one thing, but practicing them when you are upset or hurt is quite different. God wants you to live out these truths, not just know them.

(1) Romans 12:10(a); 1 Peter 1:22; 2:17; 3:8; 4:8; Hebrews 13:1

(2) Romans 12:10(b); 15:1,2; 1 Corinthians 10:24,33; Philippians 2:3,4

(3) Romans 14:19; Ephesians 4:3; 1 Peter 3:11; Hebrews 12:14

(4) Galatians 5:13; Romans 15:8

(5) Using the following passages, list some of the other great Christian virtues that should characterize your life and relationships with your brethren: Ephesians 4:1-3,32; Philippians 2:2-8; Colossians 3:12-15; Titus 3:2,3; James 3:13-18; 1 Peter 3:8,9.

b. List two virtues from the above passages that you need to improve in your personal life. Pray about this matter, but also seek practical help and advice from a mature, fellow believer. This assignment is to be done alone.

c. From the passages above, list two virtues that your congregation needs to improve upon. Read together B.E. pages 12 and 13, starting with paragraph 4 on page 12. Discuss ways in which you, the elders, could help move the congregation toward greater maturity in these weak areas.

Practical Exhortation:

Let me assure you that you will always experience some disagreement, strain, conflict, disappointment, problem, or annoyance with your fellow elders. My dearest and best friends are my fellow elders, yet we get on one another's nerves. We unintentionally hurt one another. We aren't as understanding and honest with one another as we should be. We disappoint and fail one another.

Furthermore, leaders face more stressful situations and conflicts that try their patience, humility, and love more than most people. It is much harder to be humble and loving when facing criticism and attack, or when standing up to sinful, willful people who are in the process of destroying the community. Leaders also face divisive issues and questions that King Solomon, himself, would hesitate to answer. So if you as an elder are ever to work in unity with your fellow elders, you are going to have to regularly confess your sins against your colleagues and, with the help of the Spirit, conscientiously practice the principles you have listed.

As I stated in B.E., "Yet conflict among elders remains a common and serious problem. The solution, however, is not to revert to the one-man rule. That is the easy way out. God desires that the elders humble themselves, wash one another's feet, repent, pray, turn

---

> from pride, shun impatience, and love as Christ loved. That is the kind of leadership God wants the elders to exemplify for His flock" (B.E. page 30).

7. The saints at Thessalonica were exhorted to love their hard-working leaders (verse 13). A Christian assembly should be known for its love. In one to three sentences, explain how each of the following verses shows that love should be the top priority in our theology and behavior: Matthew 22:35-40; John 13:34,35; Romans 13:10; 1 Corinthians 13:1-3; 16:14; Ephesians 5:1,2; Colossians 3:14; James 2:8; 1 Peter 4:8; 1 John 3:16,17; 4:7,8.

Practical Warning:

Many people have a strong tendency to be satisfied with mere externals—to be satisfied with outward form. If you think that elder rule and a nonclerical church structure is all that is needed to make the local church all that God intends, you are sadly mistaken. Without love, the eldership is empty. Without love, God's people will never properly grow in the grace of our Lord Jesus Christ (1 Corinthians 8:1; Ephesians 4:15,16). Without love, Christians are cold, indifferent, unbalanced, and self-centered. It is precisely because of a lack of love that we have thousands of church divisions and stand as a poor witness before a needy, watching world.

Consider carefully Francis Schaeffer's wise words of counsel from his book, *The Mark of the Christian:*

I have observed one thing among true Christians in their differences in many countries: what divides and severs true Christian groups and Christians—what leaves a bitterness that can last for 20, 30 or 40 years (or for 50 or 60 years in a son's memory)—is not the issue of

---

doctrine or belief which caused the differences in the first place. Invariably it is lack of love—and the bitter things that are said by true Christians in the midst of differences. These stick in the mind like glue. And after time passes and the differences between the Christians or the groups appear less than they did, there are still those bitter, bitter things we said in the midst of what we thought was a good and sufficient objective discussion. It is these things—these unloving attitudes and words— that cause the stench that the world can smell in the church of Jesus Christ among those who are really true Christians.

If, when we feel we must disagree as true Christians, we could simply guard our tongues and speak in love, in five or ten years the bitterness could be gone. Instead of that, we leave scars—a curse for generations. Not just a curse in the church, but a curse in the world. Newspaper headlines bear it in our Christian press, and it boils over into the secular press at times—Christians saying such bitter things about other Christians (*The Mark of the Christian,* Downers Grove: InterVarsity Press, 1970, pages 22,23).

8. a. Sing together Peter Scholtes' song, "They'll Know We Are Christians by Our Love," based on John 13:35. If you cannot find this song or don't know it, pick another song that expresses our need to love one another.

b. Pray now and ask God to help you excel even more in love for Him and His people. Pray for your congregation also, that it may abound more and more in love for all the saints. Before you pray, read together Philippians 1:9; 1 Thessalonians 3:12; 4:9,10.

SESSION SIX

PHILIPPIANS 1:1; 1 Timothy 3:1,2
(B.E. pages 204-218)

Begin Your Session by Reading These Passages:

Paul and Timothy, bond-servants of Christ Jesus, to all the saints in Christ Jesus who are in Philippi, including the overseers and deacons.

PHILIPPIANS 1:1

It is a trustworthy statement: if any man aspires to the office of overseer, it is a fine work he desires to do. An overseer, then, must be above reproach. . . .

1 TIMOTHY 3:1,2

Scripture Memory Assignment:
   1 Timothy 3:1,2.

1.   List three, unique, significant contributions Philippians 1:1 makes to our study of New Testament eldership. Explain the significance of these contributions.

2. a. The Greek term for overseers is *episkopoi.* Although it is used interchangeably for the term *elder,* explain the differences between the terms *elder* and *overseer.*

b. What connotations are conveyed by the Greek word, *episkopos*? (See B.E. page 173 for help.)

c. As you explored the Greek meaning of the word *overseer,* did you discover anything that gave you a clearer understanding of the work of the eldership? What did you discover?

d. Give two reasons why the plural use of overseer in Philippians is significant to our study.

3. a. Pages 40-44 of B.E. present three practical benefits of plurality of leadership. In your own words, summarize each of these points, then briefly discuss them together.

b. Read Exodus 18:13-23, Ecclesiastes 4:9-12, and Proverbs 24:6. List some additional advantages to collective leadership that are revealed in these passages.

c. Are you experiencing the benefits of collective leadership or do you have shared leadership in theory only, which leaves only one or two men to do all the work? What can you do to ensure that your eldership provides genuine, shared pastoral care?

d. Self-evaluation: Answer each of the following questions with "Y" for "yes" or "N" for "no" as it applies to your actions as one member of a team of overseers of God's household. Do not rush through the questions, but honestly evaluate yourself before God. Although this assignment is to be done privately, it would be helpful if another elder also answered these questions as they pertain to your behavior.

1) I act impulsively and dislike waiting on others for decisions.

2) I generally trust the judgment of my fellow elders.

3) I feel genuine concern for the interests and plans of my fellow workers.

4) I often act independently of the leadership body.

5) I make myself accountable to my fellow shepherds.

6) I work hard at cooperating with my brethren.

7) I share my burdens, fears, and problems with my fellow elders.

8) I am inclined to carry a grudge.

9) I am easily frustrated by disagreement.

10) I am afraid to honestly speak up to the group.

11) I feel free to correct and direct my fellow colleagues.

12) I actively contribute to discussions and decisions.

13) I tend to be bossy.

14) I am too sensitive.

15) I tend to dominate discussions.

16) I have a hard time apologizing or admitting I am wrong.

17) I love my fellow colleagues.

18) I consciously try to be humble and serve my fellow brethren.

19) I pray for my brothers regularly.

e. After answering these questions, ask your Father in heaven to give you a true assessment of yourself. Ask Him for the will and power to change any weaknesses or failures that are hindering the unity and love of the eldership.

4. Some typical weaknesses of shared leadership are unclear delegation of responsibilities, lack of follow through on tasks, inadequate accountability, overlapping responsibilities, and hesitancy to direct or correct one another. To solve these common problems, consider Bruce Stabbert's suggestions in appendix A for improving your corporate oversight skills. Discuss his six principles and whether they would help improve your oversight of the church.

5. Many Christians do not know that the New Testament terms *overseer, elder,* and the verb *shepherd* (pastor) all refer to the one and same body of leaders. Most Protestants think that the pastor is separate from the elders or that the bishop is separate from the pastor or elders. But few ever concern themselves with what God's holy Word actually says about these matters. It is important that you be able to articulate your view of church leadership from Scripture and give scriptural answers to those who ask or contend with you about biblical eldership. Ample evidence from the New Testament demonstrates that elders and overseers are the same body of leaders and that they have been charged by God to shepherd (pastor) the church.

Give three proofs from Scripture that the terms overseer and elder are used interchangeably and refer to the same body of leaders.

6. What connection do you see between the purpose of 1 Timothy (see 3:14,15), and the fact that 1 Timothy contains more fully developed instruction concerning eldership than any other New Testament letter?

7. George Knight refers to the saying, "It is a trustworthy statement," as "a citation-emphasis formula." Explain what that means and how it affects the saying in 1 Timothy 3:1.

8. a. The inner, spiritual desire to be an overseer of God's flock is not wrong. Indeed, it is the first logical step toward becoming an elder. Explain the differences between a right desire to be an overseer and a wrong, sinful desire.

b. *It is a most serious matter that more men will not accept the oversight responsibility of God's household.* The Lord's people are suffering because so few men care for their souls. Read the following verses and list the chief reasons why so few men have a heartfelt desire to sacrificially care for the family of God: Matthew 6:19-21,33; Luke 19:13; Romans 12:1,2; 2 Corinthians 5:15; Philippians 2:20,21; 2 Timothy 2:3,4; 4:10; James 4:4; Haggai 1:4,5; Malachi 1:6-8.

c. What steps can you as a body of leaders begin to take to solve this critical problem?

Practical Suggestions:

When I was a teenager and new Christian, I was given a book on Hudson Taylor's life, which changed my whole value system and revolutionized my outlook on life. Give the young men and women of your assembly good biographies that will challenge their hearts and minds for God. Be praying for these young people; they are the future leaders of God's work. Encourage them in the things of God and include them in some of your service to the saints. Get them involved, give them guidance, talk to them, take them to lunch, and share your burden for them. It is your job as an elder to pray and watch for laborers (Luke 10:2).

---

9. a. Explain why eldership is both an office and a work.

b. "In the face of problems and labors, *the greatest encouragement and incentive an elder can have is to know that he performs an exceedingly honorable and praiseworthy task—one that is worthy of the total sacrifice of one's life"* (B.E. page 215). Many elders become discouraged with the problems or tired of the labors, so they step aside from eldership. Young people do not sense the privilege and honor of being overseers in God's house. So it is imperative that we recapture the feelings the first Christians had toward the eldership, which is shown by their exuberant saying that church oversight is a "fine work." Develop alternative renderings or paraphrases of the clause "it is a fine work" that are meaningful to you. Other Bible translations or commentaries may help you in this task.

c. List three results of the work of the eldership that

clearly demonstrate that it is a "fine work."

10. In Philippians 1:1, the plural form of overseer was used, indicating that a team of overseers superintended the church. Explain the use of the singular form of overseer in 1 Timothy 3:2.

SESSION SEVEN

FIRST TIMOTHY 3:2-7; 5:17
(B.E. pages 218-234, 237-239)

Begin Your Session by Reading These Passages:

An overseer, then, must be above reproach, the husband of one wife, temperate, prudent, respectable, hospitable, able to teach, not addicted to wine or pugnacious, but gentle, uncontentious, free from the love of money. He must be one who manages his own household well, keeping his children under control with all dignity (but if a man does not know how to manage his own household, how will he take care of the church of God?); and not a new convert, lest he become conceited and fall into the condemnation incurred by the devil. And he must have a good reputation with those outside the church, so that he may not fall into reproach and the snare of the devil.

1 TIMOTHY 3:2-7

Let the elders who rule well be considered worthy of double honor, especially those who work hard at preaching and teaching.

1 TIMOTHY 5:17

Scripture Memory Assignment:
    1 Timothy 3:2-7.

1.   List four reasons why you think the Spirit of God emphatically insists on moral and spiritual qualifications for church elders. (Read also B.E. pages 79-81.)

2.   *Privately* evaluate how you stand with respect to each qualification. If you are really brave, ask your wife or a close friend to evaluate your standing. Write down the one number that best represents your present condition. This assignment is not meant for group discussion.

a.) A one-woman kind of man

Good		Needs Improvement		
___7___6___	|	___5___4___3___	|	___2___1___
Above Reproach				Reproachful

b.) Temperate: a stable man

Good		Needs Improvement		
___7___6___	|	___5___4___3___	|	___2___1___
Above Reproach				Reproachful

c.) Prudent: a balanced, sensible man

Good		Needs Improvement		
___7___6___	|	___5___4___3___	|	___2___1___
Above Reproach				Reproachful

d.) Respectable: an orderly, disciplined, and honorable man

Good		Needs Improvement		
___7___6___	|	___5___4___3___	|	___2___1___
Above Reproach				Reproachful

e.) Hospitable

Good		Needs Improvement	
____7____6____	|	____5____4____3____	| ____2____1____
Above Reproach			Reproachful

f.) Able to teach

Good		Needs Improvement	
____7____6____	|	____5____4____3____	| ____2____1____
Above Reproach			Reproachful

g.) Not addicted to wine

Good		Needs Improvement	
____7____6____	|	____5____4____3____	| ____2____1____
Above Reproach			Reproachful

h.) Not pugnacious

Good		Needs Improvement	
____7____6____	|	____5____4____3____	| ____2____1____
Above Reproach			Reproachful

i.) Gentle: a forbearing, gracious, and conciliatory man

Good		Needs Improvement	
____7____6____	|	____5____4____3____	| ____2____1____
Above Reproach			Reproachful

j.) Uncontentious: a peaceable man

Good		Needs Improvement	
____7____6____	|	____5____4____3____	| ____2____1____
Above Reproach			Reproachful

k.) Free from the love of money

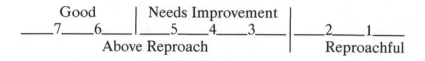

Good		Needs Improvement		
___7___6___	___5___4___3___		___2___1___
Above Reproach			Reproachful

l.) A man who manages his household well

Good		Needs Improvement		
___7___6___	___5___4___3___		___2___1___
Above Reproach			Reproachful

m.) Not a new convert

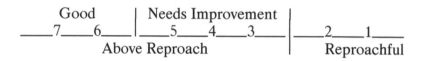

Good		Questionable		
___7___6___	___5___4___3___		___2___1___
Above Reproach			Reproachful

n.) A man with a good reputation outside the Christian community

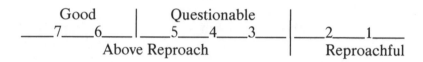

Good		Needs Improvement		
___7___6___	___5___4___3___		___2___1___
Above Reproach			Reproachful

Practical Suggestion:

Proverbs 27:17 says, "Iron sharpens iron, So one man sharpens another." True colleagues sharpen, improve, and correct each other's personal character. In the work of the Lord, moral character is supremely important. For the local church elder, personal moral and spiritual character determines one's effectiveness and influence for good. So each elder should be *highly concerned*

---

about the proper maturing of his character and correcting his faults. He must be extremely conscious of those seemingly little faults that destroy an otherwise good character: "Dead flies make a perfumer's oil stink, so a little foolishness is weightier than wisdom and honor" (Ecclesiastes 10:1). Furthermore, all of us have our blind spots that easily trip us up and frustrate our friends. So we as elders need loving criticism and correction if we expect to refine our character as Christian men.

In order to refine your character, I recommend that you seek out a fellow elder or friend you love and trust, and tell him you need his evaluation and correction. Encourage him not to be afraid to take the initiative in pointing out areas of your life that need correction and improvement. Of course it hurts to hear criticism about one's self, but you cannot develop a strong, balanced character without it. Remember, the prideful heart would rather be deceived about its true condition, but the humble mind desires truth and correction from God and fellow believers.

Read the following verses, paying careful attention to the significance of the last one: Proverbs 9:8,9; 12:1; 13:18; 15:5,12,31,32; 19:25; 27:6; 28:23; Ecclesiastes 4:13.

3. a. Note carefully the close connection between managing one's own family and managing the local church that is seen in 1 Timothy 3:5. Throughout B.E., I stated repeatedly that being a local church elder is more like being a father of a household than a leader in the military or in business. Why is that true?

b. List some ways that managing a congregation of believers differs from managing people in a business setting.

These are both very important questions, so give

some time to consider these comparisons. Note: I am not suggesting that there is no valid comparison between being a good business manager and a local church elder, for there surely is (and you could also profitably discuss those comparisons). But the New Testament stresses the family dimension of an elder's life, so this is the primary issue.

   c. What is the Greek term used for family management in verses 4 and 5? Where else is this verb used in reference to the elders' management of the church community?

Practical Exhortation:

   If you as an elder want to improve your shepherding skills, work hard at being a good father. Take a hard look at your fathering skills and interests. The vast majority of fathers give an appallingly small amount of time to guiding, counseling, playing with, or talking to their children.

   Your children are your most precious possessions (Psalm 127:3). I know how easy it is to neglect them because of overinvolvement in business, but don't. You will pay a heavy price if you do. Discipline yourself to take time with your children and talk with them. You can discover good, practical ideas from successful fathers or books about being a good father. When I meet good fathers or happy, well-adjusted teenagers, I ask questions about their home life. Pray and ask your Father in heaven to help you be enthusiastic about being a good father.

---

4. a. Why do you think hospitality is required of church elders?

   b. What does this requirement tell you about the elder's work and the nature of the church?

Practical Exhortation:

There is nothing that bonds believers together like sharing a meal together in one's home. Using your home to care for and fellowship with God's people is, I believe, one of the greatest expressions of Christian love and community (1 Peter 4:8,9). It is also a sacred privilege (Matthew 25:35,45; Hebrews 13:2).

My wife and I had been married for a year and a half when one evening she commented, "This is the first day we have been alone in our home without someone either eating a meal or staying with us!" What a holy privilege has been ours to care for and entertain the Lord's people. I believe God used our home to build our local assembly and to generate the proper Christian spirit of love and community (John 13:15). If you as a spiritual leader of God's household have closed doors, you may be responsible for coldness, unfriendliness, and lovelessness within your local fellowship. So, open your home to the Lord's people and deepen genuine, loving Christian community.

There are two additional points I would like to make in connection with hospitality, or using your home to serve Christ.

First, there is a strange expression of "Christian" love that ends at the door of the church building. People may greet you and talk to you and even appear friendly, but it goes no further than Sunday morning at a building away from home. Most often this is a sign of superficial, loveless Christianity. As leaders of the holy community, you need to address this problem. You can start to correct it by opening your own home to the Lord's people as an example of true Christian fellowship and love.

> Second, the explosive growth of small home care and study groups is one of the most significant, important trends to unite Christians together around the home and family that has occurred in the past twenty years. *Meeting in a home enhances Christian love, prayer, care, and fellowship in a way that can't happen in a church building.* As elders, I hope you encourage small home care and study groups. In our fellowship, home study and care groups have provided practical care and prayer for families that we as elders could never have accomplished on our own. These small groups have become a major help to the shepherding task. They are also an excellent training ground for future elders.

5. a. In dealing with people, problems, and profound doctrinal issues, a leader must be a balanced, sensible person, or as our text says, "prudent." A person may have intense spiritual desire, great ability, and love for God, yet be unbalanced and unsound in thinking and judgment. Such men often desire positions of spiritual leadership and prominence, but are unable to handle issues and problems sensibly, so they end up leading God's people into ugly extremes. Well-known leaders of Christian movements or institutions have caused terrible problems because they had high-blown views of themselves and were inclined to distort issues and facts and make unsound judgments. So it is vital to understand this qualification for overseers. In general terms, explain how a prudent leader would handle issues and problems differently than a man who lacked prudence.

b. Read 2 Timothy 2:24-26 and briefly outline the qualities that should characterize the Lord's servant.

66

6. a. What is the Greek word for *rule* in 1 Timothy 5:17? Write your own paraphrase of the first clause of this passage.

b. For whom do these elders (plural) provide rule? In most people's minds, who is responsible for this task?

c. The passage indicates that all elders "rule," but some "rule well." What factors make the difference?

d. Our sinful hearts are inclined toward jealousy, envy, and suspicion of one another. How does this passage help eliminate potential jealousy among fellow elders?

e. Privately read the following verses that show how prevalent and divisive the sins of jealousy and envy are among God's people: 1 Corinthians 3:3; Galatians 5:25,26; 2 Corinthians 12:20; Philippians 1:15; James 3:14,16; 1 Peter 2:1; 1 Samuel 18:6-9; Psalm 106:16; Ecclesiastes 4:4; Proverbs 27:4.

Practical Exhortation:

In Romans 12:8, the verb *prohistemi* occurs in a list of spiritual gifts. The inspired writer tells us that leading is a spiritual gift and then adds that it is to be done "with diligence" (or zeal or seriousness of purpose). Many leaders fail the Lord's people because they are half-hearted leaders; they lack zeal and wholehearted devotion to their task and to their Lord.

But our faith demands wholeheartedness, zealousness, fervency of heart, passion, and earnestness. Our Lord Himself says we are to love God with all our heart, mind, and energy, and we are to love our brethren as He has loved us (Matthew 22:37,38; John 13:34,35). Read the following passages to discover the importance of diligent service: Psalm 69:9; 2 Samuel 6:13-15; 1 Chronicles 29:3; Romans 12:11; Acts 18:25; Colossians 4:12; 1 Timothy 4:15; 2 Timothy 2:15.

> Many churches are stagnant because of *mediocrity among the leaders.* Everything is done halfheartedly: halfhearted singing, halfhearted giving, halfhearted planning, halfhearted praying, halfhearted preaching, halfhearted obedience, and halfhearted commitment.
>
> Mediocre service is a dishonor to our Lord Who poured Himself out for us—even unto death. Mediocrity also sets a poor example for young people of what Christianity is to be. So pray daily that God would help you exercise your leadership responsibility in a diligent, conscientious manner.

7. a. In the Old Testament, the elders were always a corporate leadership body. There is no suggestion that one elder was the official head of the eldership. From all that we know, the Old Testament elderships were truly corporate bodies of rulers. However, within any corporate body of rulers there are differences in talent and interest. Read carefully B.E. pages 44,45, and in your own words explain the concept of *primus inter pares.*

b. There is no proof that Peter was the president or official leader over The Twelve. Indeed, it would be false to assert such a claim. The twelve apostles formed a corporate, apostolic body with Christ as head. Yet Peter's prominence among The Twelve cannot go unnoticed. Read the following verses and explain how Peter illustrates the principle of *primus inter pares.* List Peter's specific actions that demonstrate his prominence among The Twelve: Luke 22:32; John 21:3; 20:1-8; 21:16; Acts 1:15-22; 2:14; 3:1-6,12; 4:7,8; 5:2,3,8,15,29; 8:14,20; 15:7; Galatians 2:7-14. (Note also John's place of prominence among The Twelve.)

8. Since most people don't know what genuine, shared

68

leadership is, they inevitably want to know who leads the elders. Read again the profound quotation by Robert Girard on page 10 and write out how you would answer this question.

Practical Suggestions:

Since the eldership seeks Christ's leading through His Spirit, and because no individual elder has any legal or official status over the others, the elders should seek a unanimous consensus on all major decisions.

A number of times I have seen a decision or proposal that was agreed to by the majority of elders rightly postponed because one elder disagreed. The Spirit of God used the one brother to stop the rest of the eldership from making a mistake. I have also seen the opposite occur, when one brother incorrectly objected to an idea agreeable to the rest. In time, however, God brought unanimity to the eldership. Remember, we desire Christ's will, not our own will that is often flawed. So the body of elders is required to depend on God and patiently pray for one another.

In minor matters, it is normally good to try to encourage or defer to one another's plans or ideas, even if you as an individual elder don't fully agree. If one or two elders are burdened about something or want to try something that you don't necessarily agree with, it is appropriate to express your concern or disagreement. But after expressing your concern, it may well be appropriate to concede for the sake of unity and brotherly love. As elders, we should do all we can to cooperate and encourage one another, even if a particular action is not our preference. A true, humble, servant spirit seeks the interest and concerns of others.

A self-willed man offers little hope for cooperation and brotherly accord.

9. a. Great leaders and teachers also have great faults; only Jesus Christ is perfect. Peter is a prime example of a great leader who had great faults. How does a plurality of leadership help multigifted, charismatic leaders become better leaders?

b. What kinds of sins or failures do exceptionally talented leaders fall prey to if they don't have colleagues to interact with on an equal basis?

10. There will always be the temptation to let one, talented, energetic person do all the work (B.E. pages 46,47). Together talk about specific steps or procedures you can take to assure that all elders—not just one man—are functioning as shepherds. Of course you may not have a multigifted, dynamic person among you—few churches do, but the problem of leaving all the work to one conscientious person is still common.

SESSION EIGHT

FIRST TIMOTHY 5:17,18
(B.E. pages 239-241, 246-252)

Begin Your Session by Reading This Passage:

Let the elders who rule well be considered worthy of double honor, especially those who work hard at preaching and teaching. For the Scripture says, "You shall not muzzle the ox while he is threshing," and "The laborer is worthy of his wages."

1 TIMOTHY 5:17,18

Scripture Memory Assignment:
1 Timothy 5:17,18.

1. a. The elders singled out for special mention (note carefully the meaning of the adverb, *especially*) are those who "work hard at preaching and teaching." What Greek verb is used here for "work hard"? What does it mean?

b. Explain in specific terms how the apostle can say preaching and teaching are "hard work."

c. Note the close connection between leading and teaching in 1 Timothy 5:17. In what sense does one who teaches the Word also lead?

2. a. One of the most serious problems in churches today is the lack of solid Bible teaching. Many teachers give only 20-minute sermonettes on Sunday morning. This is not enough food for the flock. Thus, the people are weak and unprincipled, and few men qualify to be elders because of their lack of knowledge. Although such a church may grow numerically, it is immature and underdeveloped in spiritual life and knowledge. Using Ephesians 4:11,12, explain the significant task the spiritually gifted teacher has in developing the Lord's people.

 b. Discuss together the Bible teaching ministry of your church and how you can improve it. Don't be passive or neglect this issue. The spiritual welfare of the people depends on it. Are gifted teachers teaching the Word or are they giving simple sermonettes each week? Are those who teach unedifying and dull? As overseers of the household of God, you have every right to ask these questions and evaluate the teaching ministry. Moreover, those who minister the Word publicly need your counsel and evaluation.

Practical Suggestion:
 Many Christians don't know the basics of their faith. New converts and immature believers need to be taught the fundamentals of the faith: God, Christ, Scripture, Gospel, Christian living, etc. Your church's teaching ministry needs to include basic teaching for new and immature believers. You need a regular class on the foundations of the faith to get believers started on a solid foundation of truth. If you are a teacher of the Word, don't neglect to teach new babies in Christ because you personally prefer to teach new material to mature believers.

---

3. a. Ephesians 4:11 speaks of the gifted person called

shepherd (pastor). Describe what this gift is.

b. How is this person (the shepherd) different from the gifted teacher? (Read carefully note #17 B.E. page 264.)

c. Why would the gift of shepherding be of special importance to the eldership?

d. Today it is almost universally accepted that the gift of shepherding is the same thing as the office of pastor, which is an office separate from and above the elders. How would you show from Scripture that this is a false concept?

4. Below is a list of spiritual gifts that would have particular relevance to making the eldership an effective shepherding team. Explain how each gift would generally make the eldership more effective, and how your eldership specifically would use such gifts.

a. Administrations (1 Corinthians 12:28). The Greek term for *administrations* (*kybernesis*) is literally steering or piloting a ship. Originally it depicted the action of a helmsman (Greek, *kybernetes*). Here, however, it is used figuratively for governing, administrating, or guiding a society of believers.

Look up Proverbs 11:14 and 24:6, where this same term appears for *guidance,* and explain its importance to the congregation.

b. Leading (Romans 12:8). This is the Greek word, *prohistemi,* that we have noted several times already. You may want to refer back to the exposition of 1 Thessalonians (B.E. pages 198-200).

c. Exhortation (Romans 12:8).

d. Teachers (Ephesians 4:11).

e. Shepherd (Ephesians 4:11).

f. Evangelists (Ephesians 4:11).

g. Mercy (Romans 12:8).

h. Giving (Romans 12:8).

5. a. Draw a chart that looks something like the one in Appendix B, with the appropriate number of squares for each elder in your church. Together, discuss the gifts and duties of each elder until the whole chart is filled in. There are more spiritual gifts than those listed above (see Romans 12:3-8; 1 Corinthians 12; 1 Peter 4:11).
   b. Privately, list what contributions—in interest, personality, time, talent, etc.—you make to the eldership. Do not discuss this in the group session.

Practical Suggestions:
   The role of moderator (or chairman) in the elders' meetings is highly important. The moderator exercises considerable control over the direction and efficiency of the meetings. Since a good deal of attention is focused on him during the meeting, considerable thought should be given to who the moderator should be.
   If a brother is exceptionally talented at leading and organizing, it might be best to let him moderate the meetings. Another option is to give the responsibility to each elder for a three- to six-month period (assuming weekly meetings). Also, I urge you *to have a written job description for the moderator.* Whatever method you choose, substantial thought and continual evaluation should go into this position of responsibility.
   Periodically you should evaluate the tone, order, emphasis, time, and atmosphere of your elders' meetings. Since your meetings together are vital, you should always try to improve their efficiency and character.

---

6. It is important to understand that gifted teachers, exhorters, evangelists, and leaders are greatly used of God to start churches, win people to Christ, and build up the Lord's people, but they are not all church elders. Local elderships should seek the services of such gifted men, particularly if they themselves are not gifted with an evangelist or teacher.

Discuss the spiritual gift(s) of the following four men and how their gifts could help a local church: (a) Apollos (Acts 18:27; 1 Corinthians 3:5-9; 16:12); (b) Epaphras (Colossians 1:5-8; 4:12,13); (c) Timothy (1 Corinthians 16:10; 1 Thessalonians 3:2,6; 2 Timothy 4:5); and (d) Barnabas (Acts 11:19-26).

Practical Suggestion:

Paul, the wisest of all church builders, knew that the believers at Corinth needed help, so he urged Apollos to go to Corinth (1 Corinthians 16:12; cf. Acts 18:27,28). Do not allow pride to prevent you from seeking help from gifted teachers, shepherds, and leaders of Christ's body; their gift is for the *whole* body of Christ, not just one local congregation.

Barnabas knew that Paul's extraordinary gifts would be invaluable to the new congregation at Antioch, so "he left for Tarsus to look for Saul; and when he had found him, he brought him to Antioch" (Acts 11:25,26). Most men would have been threatened to bring such a spiritual giant into the work. But Barnabas, faithful to his name, was concerned about the Lord's people—not his own ego or status. As shepherds, the elders must seek the best help available for the spiritual welfare of the flock.

---

7. a. Using 1 Timothy 5:1-16, explain from the context why the word *honor* (Greek, *time*) must include the sense of material provision.

b. The scriptural quotations in 1 Timothy 5:18, from

both the Old and New Testaments, refer to material provision for workers. What is the inspired writer's purpose for using these two quotations?

c. Whose responsibility is it to see that "double honor" is rendered to the elders?

d. Look up Galatians 6:6 and explain how it applies to the previous question.

Practical Suggestions:

If an elder receives material provision from the congregation, it is essential that there be clear and open understanding about the elder's responsibility and service to his fellow brethren.

Whenever money is involved, the potential for conflict and problems heightens. So, it is imperative that there be good communication between those who give and those who receive. I have seen gifted teachers who spent so much time traveling to other churches to speak that the home congregation became upset. The people felt slighted by the man they supported to serve their congregation. Such problems can be solved by simply talking about what each person expects from the other and making appropriate adjustments of priorities and funds.

Two truths must be kept in balance when we consider the financial support of elders or missionaries. First, the worker is the Lord's servant and is ultimately accountable to Him. At the same time, he is the servant of his brethren and lives in mutual, loving dependence and accountability within a community of saints. The idea of a servant who is both independent and unaccountable is a contradiction. In our congregation, we have found that the best policy is direct and *consistent* communication with all whom we financially support.

> We strive for a spirit of close partnership in the Lord's work. This cannot occur without agreement and clear understanding on all sides.

8. a. How is the eldership strengthened by having an elder(s) serve in a full- or part-time capacity? List at least three ways.

    b. List two serious pitfalls an eldership must guard against if one of its members serves in the shepherding work full or part time.

Practical Suggestions:

If you serve the congregation in a full-time capacity, here are a few words of counsel:

(1) Guard yourself from wasting time or being lazy. Don't work at your task any less than your fellow elders. If they get up early every day to go to work and then serve the assembly in the evenings, don't you do anything less. If you are not an example of discipline and diligence, your brothers will eventually resent you and there will be problems between you.

(2) Do not permit your fellow elders to give all the work of the church to you. Shared oversight means exactly that—shared work. Do not be afraid to delegate work to your colleagues, to say you will take on a task only if they help you, or to just say "no." Be open about this matter. Talk frankly about your fears that others will not take their responsibility seriously. If you do all the work, then you do not have a true, biblical eldership. You only have a theory.

(3) If you are a teacher and a strong public figure, you will need to take steps to lower your public profile and encourage others in public matters. You don't need

to make every pronouncement, pray at every function, put your name on every publication, or be on every committee. The truly great leader wants to promote and advance others, not just himself.

(4) Remember, your personal example of Christian character is your most important asset and enduring legacy.

SESSION NINE

FIRST TIMOTHY 5:19-25
(B.E. pages 252-262)

Begin Your Session by Reading This Passage:

Do not receive an accusation against an elder except on the basis of two or three witnesses. Those who continue in sin, rebuke in the presence of all, so that the rest also may be fearful of sinning. I solemnly charge you in the presence of God and of Christ Jesus and of His chosen angels, to maintain these principles without bias, doing nothing in a spirit of partiality. Do not lay hands upon anyone too hastily and thus share responsibility for the sins of others; keep yourself free from sin. No longer drink water exclusively, but use a little wine for the sake of your stomach and your frequent ailments. The sins of some men are quite evident, going before them to judgment; for others, their sins follow after. Likewise also, deeds that are good are quite evident, and those which are otherwise cannot be concealed.

1 TIMOTHY 5:19-25

Scripture Memory Assignment:
    1 Timothy 5:19-25.

79

1. a. Elders who are genuinely involved with people's problems and sins will eventually make enemies—count on it! Angry, sinful, distorted people will make wild accusations if their sins are rebuked or exposed by the elders (1 Samuel 24:9; 3 John 10). How would you apply Amos 5:10 to yourself and the previous statement?

   b. How should the congregation and its leaders respond to accusations against an elder?

2. As an elder, you will be called on to make judgments between people. This is a difficult job in an unjust world. When it comes to relatives and close friends, the best Christian people are guilty of bias or believing only one side of a story. Read the following verses prayerfully and write a one- or two-sentence summary of each. Together, have each elder read his summary of one or two verses until you have covered every verse. You will want to memorize some of these verses because they will guide you and protect you in your daily work with people. Proverbs 18:13,17; 21:15(a); 24:23; Leviticus 19:15; Deuteronomy 16:20; 2 Chronicles 19:6,7; Job 29:16; Isaiah 61:8(a); John 7:51.

Practical Suggestions:
   Keep records whenever you are involved in judging a dispute or in cases of church discipline. I have saved myself from serious misunderstandings and false accusations a number of times by having accurate records of phone conversations, dates, testimonies, and events. On several occasions I was able to produce facts and records, that I myself had forgotten, for people who questioned how our church handled the discipline of members who later accused us of mishandling their situation (a charge every unrepentant sinner makes against those who confront and deal with their sin). In highly delicate and

---

unpleasant situations that demand the judgment and counsel of the elders, it is all too easy to forget what was said and what was decided. Indeed, all decisions and judgments made by the elders should be accurately recorded so that valuable time is not wasted in trying to remember past decisions.

3. a. What is talebearing and why is it so destructive to a community?

b. In contrast to talebearing, which qualities should characterize an elder? The following verses will help you answer this question: Proverbs 11:13; 16:28; 17:9; 18:8; 20:19; 26:20; Ecclesiastes 10:20; Ephesians 4:29; James 1:26.

4. a. Although our Lord Himself and His apostles plainly instructed how to discipline sinning members of the body, church discipline is almost unheard of in evangelical churches. This has resulted in terrible dishonor to Christ and weak churches. Why do you think Christian churches refuse to practice this teaching? The following Scriptures will help you consider this question:

    (1) 1 Corinthians 5:2;

    (2) Psalm 81:11; Jeremiah 7:28; 1 Samuel 15:22;

    (3) 1 Samuel 2:29,30; John 12:43;

    (4) Isaiah 5:21; Proverbs 3:7; 26:12;

    (5) Proverbs 29:25; Deuteronomy 1:17;

    (6) Ezra 10:4; 2 Chronicles 15:7,8; 32:7;

    (7) Revelation 3:19;

    (8) Isaiah 66:2.

Also refer to B.E. pages 114,115.

b. Read together the following quotation by John Knox and discuss how it applies to the practice of church discipline in 99 percent of evangelical churches today. Does it apply to your body of believers?

Supposing that contemplating the good is the same as being good; that we are less selfish because we admire unselfishness; that we are less proud because we admire humility. . . . In the same way one may feel that to confess one is selfish is as good as being unselfish, that to admit one is proud or lustful is as good as being poor in spirit or chaste; that one achieves virtue by paying tribute and acknowledging one's lack of it.

5. Why must a sinning elder be publicly exposed and rebuked before the entire congregation?

Practical Exhortation:

An internationally renowned statesman was asked, "What is the most important quality for a national leader to possess?" He answered, "Courage."

Confronting and rebuking a fellow elder (or anyone else) who is sinning requires a courageous spirit. If you lack courage to exercise church discipline, which most of us do, read prayerfully the following Scriptures and pray for courage and strength: Exodus 1:15-21; Joshua 1:6-9; 1 Samuel 17:32-37; 2 Samuel 10:12; 1 Kings 2:1,2; 18:3,4; 1 Chronicles 28:20; 2 Chronicles 32:4-8; Ezra 10:4; Ezekiel 2:6,7; Daniel 1:8-13; 3:12,16-18,28; 6:10; Amos 7:10-17; Haggai 2:4.

---

6. a. One of the most difficult things elders ever have to do is remove an elder who wants to remain in office, but obviously does not belong. Yet this painful task must be done. List three serious problems your eldership will face if you do not remove an unfit or sinful elder (B.E. pages 86-89).

b. If you believed that one of your fellow elders did not qualify to be an elder, how would you personally deal with the problem? List specific steps.

7. One unfit elder can cause untold trouble for a church and bring havoc on an eldership. So, in order to prevent unqualified and unworthy men from entering the eldership, the Spirit of God gives invaluable counsel to the body of believers. Using the following texts, explain what Scripture says concerning prospective elders.

a. 1 Timothy 5:22 (cf. Proverbs 19:2; 21:5). What possible consequences await those who neglect this injunction?

b. 1 Timothy 3:10. Since the Greek text is quite abbreviated, write an expanded paraphrase of this verse.

c. Explain how each of the following statements from 1 Timothy 5:24,25 encourage and guide the local church and its elders in examining potential elders.

(1) "The sins of some men are quite evident, going before them to judgment."

(2) "For others, their sins follow after."

(3) "Likewise also, deeds that are good are quite evident."

(4) "and those which are otherwise cannot be concealed."

Practical Suggestion:

We involve the congregation in evaluating a prospective elder by giving each member a survey listing the qualifications of an elder. This encourages the congregation to think and pray about a man's suitability—not just rely on the elders' judgment. If some believers have scriptural reservations about a candidate, the elders seek to find out what those reservations are. If you desire, you can make a survey of qualifications by using the evaluation charts presented in sessions 8 and 13.

---

8. a. What wrong tendencies must you guard against and warn the congregation about when considering a new elder? This is a very important question! Good men have been unjustly refused the responsibility of church oversight, which has been detrimental to the local church (B.E. page 346).

b. Talk about how you as an eldership can improve the process of evaluating prospective elders. God's Spirit leaves these matters to the discretion of the local church, thus the Scripture is silent.

c. How would you counsel a man who wants to be an elder, but is considered to be unqualified by the church and elders? (See B.E. pages 350-352 for help.)

9. Why is an official, public installation of elders and deacons important to the church and its officers (Acts 6:6; 14:23)?

10. List and discuss three reasons (see chapter 18 of B.E.) why ordination in the modern, ecclesiastical sense of the word is an unscriptural doctrine.

Practical Suggestion:
 Local, state, and federal governments have certain legal requirements for churches and their officials regarding marriage ceremonies, taxation benefits, representation, etc. Since Christians are to cooperate as much as possible with the state (Matthew 22:21; Romans 13:1-7), most of these legal considerations can be easily fulfilled by appointing one or two of the elders as legal representatives of the church. These elders could be licensed to perform marriage ceremonies and visit jails if the state requires it. Most governments are broad enough in their definition of ordination to

---

include those of us who reject the traditional Protestant and Catholic definitions of ordination. Our local assembly has found that we are able to fulfill our government's requirements fully and with good conscience without affecting our church government.

I highly recommend that you have copies of the government regulations and tax laws regarding religious organizations, and that the eldership carefully study them so that your church can comply in good conscience or intelligently object to the existing laws.

SESSION TEN

TITUS 1:5-10; JAMES 5:14,15
(B.E. pages 265-281; 283-293)

Begin Your Session by Reading These Passages:

For this reason I left you in Crete, that you might set in order what remains, and appoint elders in every city as I directed you, namely, if any man be above reproach, the husband of one wife, having children who believe, not accused of dissipation or rebellion. For the overseer must be above reproach as God's steward, not self-willed, not quick-tempered, not addicted to wine, not pugnacious, not fond of sordid gain, but hospitable, loving what is good, sensible, just, devout, self-controlled, holding fast the faithful word which is in accordance with the teaching, that he may be able both to exhort in sound doctrine and to refute those who contradict. For there are many rebellious men, empty talkers and deceivers, especially those of the circumcision, who must be silenced because they are upsetting whole families, teaching things they should not teach, for the sake of sordid gain.

TITUS 1:5-10

Is anyone among you sick? Let him call for the elders of the church, and let them pray over him, anointing

87

*him with oil in the name of the Lord; and the prayer
offered in faith will restore the one who is sick, and the
Lord will raise him up, and if he has committed sins, they
will be forgiven him.*

JAMES 5:14,15

Scripture Memory Assignment:
  Titus 1:5-10.

1. a. What did Paul think of churches that did not have officially appointed elders?

  b. Write your own paraphrase and explain the significance of the words, "as I directed you, namely, if any man be. . . ."

2. a. What is the inspired writer's reason for interjecting the statement, "For the overseer must be above reproach as God's steward" (verse 7), in the midst of listing the qualifications of an elder?

  b. Who is the overseer in verse 7?

  c. What does the appearance of the term *overseer* in verse 7 prove?

3. a. What does the Greek term for *steward* mean?

  b. What significant truths should both the congregation and the elders grasp by the connection of the word *God* with *steward*?

  c. What does the term *steward* tell us about the elders' work and identity?

Practical Suggestions:
  Since the elders are the overseers and stewards of God's household, it is best that they also be the legal trustees of your church corporation. It is best not to

---

have a separate, legal board, for this could lead to a power struggle. If the elders are the God-placed stewards of the Christian household, they should also be the stewards of the legal corporation and its holdings. It would be wise to state this point in the bylaws of your corporation.

I have four additional suggestions concerning the bylaws of your corporation: they should assert that the Bible is your constitution, they should be short and simple, they should be easy to amend when desired, and they should explain the governmental structure of your church. It is best not to use the term *constitution* for your bylaws, because for most people a constitution is a revered document that is not readily amended. The Bible is our true constitution, and I do not say that in a sanctimonious or impractical way.

4. a. Carefully read and meditate upon Numbers 12:7, "'Not so, with My servant Moses, He is faithful in all My household.'" As a steward of God's household, how does this verse affect your thinking about yourself and God?

b. How does the concept of faithfulness affect your thinking about your work as God's steward? Read the following verses and write down some observations to share with the other elders. 1 Samuel 22:14; 2 Chronicles 19:8,9; Nehemiah 7:2; Proverbs 20:6; 25:19; Daniel 6:4; Luke 12:42-44,48; 1 Corinthians 4:2; 1 Timothy 1:12; 2 Timothy 2:2; Hebrews 3:6; 1 Peter 4:10; 3 John 5.

5. Privately evaluate how you stand with respect to each qualification below. (See page 60 for further instructions.)

a.) Not self-willed

Good	Needs Improvement	
___7___6___ | ___5___4___3___	| ___2___1___
Above Reproach	Reproachful

b.) Not quick-tempered

Good	Needs Improvement	
___7___6___ | ___5___4___3___	| ___2___1___
Above Reproach	Reproachful

c.) Loving what is good

Good	Needs Improvement	
___7___6___ | ___5___4___3___	| ___2___1___
Above Reproach	Reproachful

d.) Just

Good	Needs Improvement	
___7___6___ | ___5___4___3___	| ___2___1___
Above Reproach	Reproachful

e.) Devout

Good	Needs Improvement	
___7___6___ | ___5___4___3___	| ___2___1___
Above Reproach	Reproachful

f.) Self-controlled

Good	Needs Improvement	
___7___6___ | ___5___4___3___	| ___2___1___
Above Reproach	Reproachful

90

g.) Committed to the Word of God

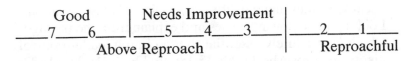

h.) Able to exhort in sound doctrine

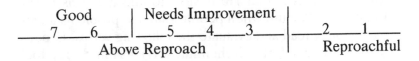

i.) Able to refute opponents

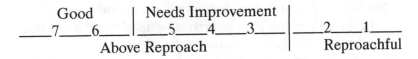

> **Practical Warning:**
> Leaders of God's household must meet God's requirements for office, yet we must guard against perfectionistic thinking. All elders have feet of clay; we all have weaknesses and faults; we are not super saints. Indeed, the longer we live and work together, the more apparent our shortcomings become. Idealistic thinking about people is destructive. We must remember that God's power and glory are displayed through our weaknesses, inabilities, difficulties, and shortcomings (1 Corinthians 2:3-5; 4:7-12; 12:9,10).

6. a. A quick-tempered man is always a problem to the eldership and the church. That is why a quick-tempered man cannot be an elder. Anger must always be controlled and channeled properly. This is especially true of an elder because he must handle difficult people and tense situations. Look up the following verses and explain from the passages why it is absolutely essential that a church leader control his anger. Proverbs 14:29; 15:18; 16:32; 19:11; 29:8,11,22; Ephesians 4:26,27; James 1:19,20.

b. One of God's attributes that should gladden and comfort our hearts is that He is slow to anger. Let us never forget this attribute when people's sin and problems anger us. Privately read and evaluate the following verses: Exodus 34:6; Numbers 14:18; Nehemiah 9:17; Psalm 86:15; Joel 2:13; Jonah 4:2; Nahum 1:3.

7. a. An elder must be characterized by "holding fast" to the Word of God. What does this term mean?

b. What does this characteristic tell us about the attitude an elder should have toward God's Word?

c. Job was an elder. What was his attitude toward God's precious Word (Job 23:11,12)?

d. What was the Psalmist's attitude toward God's Word (Psalm 119:97,127,136,162,163)?

e. What was Paul's attitude concerning Scripture (2 Timothy 3:15-17)?

8. Elders must be men of Scripture. If not, the flock will suffer. Titus 1:9 sets forth specific duties required of elders. What two things must elders be able to do with the "faithful word"? Give a brief two-or three-sentence explanation of each of these responsibilities.

Practical Exhortation:
God's stewards must be humble, loving, and forbearing. Yet at times they must also fight. Elders must

---

be assertive and quick to move, or the flock will be ravished (Acts 15:1,2).

I have seen churches ruined because local leaders waited too long to act against problems or false teaching. Our Lord was humble and serving, yet He vigorously confronted the false religious leaders of His day. He even confronted faithlessness and selfishness among His disciples. If you are a leader, you have to confront people and take action against sinful behavior. At times you must be tough or you will fail and the household of God will suffer as a result of your inaction and fear. In Titus 1:9-11 elders are required to silence and reprove those involved in false teaching. As leaders of God's people, in a world bent on lies and idols, take careful note of Aaron's failure (Exodus 32:21-25).

9. a. What are some practical benefits, to both the sick person and the elders, of praying at the bedside of the sick rather than at another location?

b. In what ways does James assume that elders must be men of strong faith and prayer?

Practical Exhortation:

Prayer is a major part of the work of the Lord, especially for those who lead the Lord's people (Acts 6:4). Elders often face agonizing and perplexing situations that demand guidance from the Lord; they encounter opposition from their brethren and outside forces, minister to weak and struggling believers, and care for the hurting and needy. All of these things require prayer for strength and wisdom. As a spiritual leader, where do you see the priority of prayer in your life?

10. a. What aspect of the shepherding task is expressed by James 5?

b. How does this injunction show that biblical eldership is not just another church organizational board?

c. What in this passage specifically shows that elders must have the tender skill to deal with people in the areas of sin and restoration?

11. a. The application of oil to the sick is a practice that has long been debated. What is the main thrust of James' counsel?

b. What are the two, main, contending views regarding the application of oil to the sick by the elders? Explain why you hold the position you do.

12. A sure sign of a weak, ineffective eldership is a lack of attention to the basic duty of praying for the sick (Ezekiel 34:4; Matthew 25:36,39,40). If you as a body of elders believe that you have been negligent in practicing this biblical injunction, talk about how you will remedy this failure. Remember, you will have to teach the saints concerning this subject or they will never call upon you.

Practical Suggestions:

When the elders of our assembly are called to a home to pray for a sick person, our practice has been:

(1) To bring along song books and sing appropriate songs, which sets a good atmosphere for prayer and seeking the Lord.

(2) Each elder in turn shares a Scripture portion and word of encouragement and counsel with the one who is sick and his or her family, if present. During this time, one of the elders may lovingly ask about the person's relationship to the Lord and if there is unconfessed sin. (We have not experienced any adverse reaction

---

to this question. Most sick people who call for the elders are willing to face their relationship to the Lord honestly.)

(3) One of the elders applies oil on the one who is sick, if requested.

(4) We all kneel and pray. Each of us will pray once, and some of us will pray two or three times.

(5) One or two of the elders will hold the hand of the one who is sick, communicating our love and affection.

SESSION ELEVEN

FIRST PETER 5:1-3
(B.E. pages 295-305)

Begin Your Session by Reading This Passage:

Therefore, I exhort the elders among you, as your fellow elder and witness of the sufferings of Christ, and a partaker also of the glory that is to be revealed, shepherd the flock of God among you, exercising oversight not under compulsion, but voluntarily, according to the will of God; and not for sordid gain, but with eagerness; nor yet as lording it over those allotted to your charge, but proving to be examples to the flock.

1 PETER 5:2-6

Scripture Memory Assignment:
    1 Peter 5:1-3.

1. a. There is a deep sense of urgency to this passage. Give two major reasons why you think Peter was moved to give this urgent exhortation to the elders of the churches of Asia Minor.

   b. Do you feel any sense of urgency about your task of shepherding the flock? If so, what arouses your sense of urgency?

c. Make a list of the things, attitudes, or activities that hinder you from carrying out the urgent task of caring for the Lord's people.

d. As a group, pray now about the hindrances to your ministry of shepherding God's people.

Practical Exhortation:

Sloth and inattentiveness to the local flock of God is a prevalent problem in churches around the world. If the kind of attention many shepherds give to their churches were given to literal flocks, the sheep would have died a long time ago.

If you are an inattentive shepherd, you have two options. One is to step aside from your office. The other, and better option, is to confess your failure and renew your commitment to the Lord and His people: "The solution to the problem of elders' inattentiveness and sloth is their renewed obedience to the Holy Spirit's urgent, imperative command for elders to be all that a shepherd should be in caring for God's flock." (B.E. pages 120,121).

Please understand that renewal, reform, and revitalization are continuous tasks for all churches and individual Christians. The church at Ephesus was doctrinally sound and had endured persecution and affliction, yet the Lord called it to repent and renew its first love: "'Remember therefore from where you have fallen, and repent and do the deeds you did at first; or else I am coming to you, and will remove your lampstand out of its place— unless you repent'" (Revelation 2:5). The nation of Israel constantly needed reform and revival. So if you need to renew your love and service for the Lord's people, remember that it is a task all of us have had to do a number of times.

Peter's charge to the elders is to shepherd the churches of God as they should. Since elders are to shepherd the flock of God, it is essential to carefully study the characteristics of a good, Palestinian shepherd. This assignment (numbers two through five) is to be done privately.

2. *The shepherd's presence.* In the ancient Near East, shepherding entailed being with the sheep. There was a real relationship between the sheep and the shepherd. Amazingly, the shepherd's presence made all the difference in the world to the sheep. They knew him and followed him. His presence brought peace and security to the sheep: "'the sheep hear his voice, and he calls his own sheep by name, and leads them out . . . the sheep follow him because they know his voice . . . the good shepherd lays down His life for the sheep . . . I am the good shepherd, and I know My own, and My own know Me'" (John 10:3,4,11,14).

God's people instinctively know who really cares for and loves them. They know who the shepherds are. They respond to the shepherds' voice and leading. The shepherds' very presence in the flock makes all the difference; it is a reality that can be felt psychologically, emotionally, and spiritually. The shepherds' presence is essential to the well-being of the church. Good shepherds, then, love to be with the sheep.

a. Evaluate your shepherding task in terms of the time you spend with the people. Do not include attendance at regular Sunday meetings; count only the time you spend on the phone, meeting with others, joint family activities, or other occasions that demonstrate your presence with the saints as a shepherd and lover of the sheep. Write down the number that best represents your involvement with the people.

(1) One hour or less a week
(2) Two to five hours a week

(3) Five hours or more a week

(4) Ten hours or more a week

b. If you find that you are a Sunday-morning-only shepherd, list two specific things you can start doing on a regular basis that will put you into direct, consistent contact with the people. The people desperately need your loving attention, so pray that God will give you a passion to be with them and to be concerned for them.

3. *Love for sheep.* In ancient Palestine, a good shepherd was characterized by his love for his sheep. Love is one of the most beautiful qualities of Palestinian shepherds. Second Samuel 12:3 describes one poor Palestinian man who "'. . . had nothing except one little ewe lamb Which he had bought and nourished; And it grew up together with him and his children. It would eat of his bread and drink of his cup and lie in his bosom, And was like a daughter to him.'"

King David, who loved his people, likened them to sheep: "And David said to God, 'Is it not I who commanded to count the people? Indeed, I am the one who has sinned and done very wickedly, but these sheep, what have they done? O Lord my God, please let Thy hand be against me and my father's household, but not against Thy people that they should be plagued'" (1 Chronicles 21:17).

In Isaiah 40:11, God is likened to a shepherd who loves his sheep: "Like a shepherd He will tend His flock, In His arm He will gather the lambs, And carry them in His bosom; He will gently lead the nursing ewes" (cf. Ezekiel 34:11-16). The Great Shepherd, the Lord Jesus, also loved His sheep and laid down His life for them (John 10:11).

a. Evaluate your love for the flock. Would you sacrifice for them, serve them, go out of your way for them, suffer discomfort for them, die for them? List some specific ways in which you love God's people. Remember, if you do not

100

love the Lord's people, you will never be a good pastor.

b. Remember, too, that love is an active word. It is easy to say you love the people, but genuine love produces deeds as well as words. Genuine love motivates one to actions such as consistent prayer for the saints, home visitation, counseling, alertness to problems, sensitivity to needs, practical care, or seeking out straying sheep. Which of your deeds or attitudes as an elder best demonstrate your love for the people?

c. Look up the following verses and briefly explain how each of these saints showed deeds of love for God's people. 1 Corinthians 16:15; Colossians 4:12,13; Philemon 5,7; 3 John 5,6.

d. Do you experience any particular attitudes or feelings toward people that make you question the genuineness of your love for the saints of God? What are they? Your answer should be kept between you and the Lord so you will answer honestly. Pray over your areas of weakness, thanking God for the love you have and asking Him for a fresh passion of love for His people.

4. *Knowledge and skill.* A good shepherd knows sheep and understands the land. The well-being of the flock depends on the shepherd's knowledge of sheep and land and his skillful management of both. If the land is destroyed by overuse or the water supply is endangered, the sheep will suffer. A skilled shepherd always has an eye out for his sheep. He knows their needs, when something is wrong, if one is missing, if one is in trouble, and he knows each one's peculiarities. Like King David, a good shepherd is skillful and wise: "He also chose David His servant, And took him from the sheepfolds; From the care of the ewes with sucking lambs He brought him, To shepherd Jacob His people, And Israel His inheritance. So he shep-

LINCOLN CHRISTIAN COLLEGE AND SEMINARY

herded them according to the integrity of his heart, And guided them with his skillful hands" (Psalm 78:70-72). What a critical need there is for men with wise, skillful, shepherding hands!

Likewise, a good elder knows people. He knows how sensitive they are and knows their needs, their troubles, their weaknesses, their sins, and their hearts. He knows how people can hurt one another. He also knows how to handle people with patience, wisdom, and a tender heart. Furthermore, he knows how stubborn and exasperating they can sometimes be. Paul's second letter to the Corinthians is an example *par excellence* of a shepherd who skillfully leads, corrects, rebukes, and cares for his rebellious, misled flock.

A major part of the eldership's task is to persuade people, moving them in new directions, making changes, correcting attitudes, and raising their horizons. It is not easy to move people onward and upward; most love their comfort zones. Furthermore, the elders must always be planning for future needs, problems, and demands so that the flock will always have the sustenance it needs.

Thus, foresight is one of the most important qualities of a good leader. As shepherds and overseers of the flock of God, the elders must take time to plan and think about the flock's future needs and direction (Proverbs 21:5(a)). If you as a body of elders do not know how to plan ahead, then seek outside help from other churches or Christian leaders. Don't allow yourselves to do nothing until the flock is endangered.

a. As a shepherd, identify areas of responsibility within your congregation that need more planning and forethought. Discuss these needs together.

5. *Hard work.* Shepherding is constant work; sheep do

102

not take vacations from eating and drinking, nor do predators vanish. So shepherding is hard work, sometimes requiring long hours of work under uncomfortable conditions. Jacob is a good example of a hard-working shepherd: "These twenty years I have been with you; your ewes and your female goats have not miscarried, nor have I eaten the rams of your flocks. That which was torn of beasts I did not bring to you; I bore the loss of it myself. You required it of my hand whether stolen by day or stolen by night. Thus I was: by day the heat consumed me, and the frost by night, and my sleep fled from my eyes" (Genesis 31:38-40).

a. One essential requirement of a good shepherd of God's people is a willing spirit to work hard and devote long hours to the task. List the qualities you see in Jacob that make a good shepherd.

6. a. In summary form, list the chief characteristics of a good Palestinian shepherd from the above assignment. Discuss your findings with the group, then do the same for the next three questions.

b. List one characteristic of a shepherd that is a personal weakness in your ministry.

c. List one characteristic of a shepherd that is a personal strength in your ministry.

d. As an eldership, what are your weakest and strongest characteristics in shepherding the flock?

Practical Suggestion:
You cannot shepherd a flock or watch over the souls of the Lord's people without knowing the people. You cannot know the people without visiting their homes, talking with them and asking about their spiritual lives. I believe that home visitation is absolutely essential to shepherding care.

---

7. a. Explain why the phrase "of God," used to describe flock, should highly motivate you in your task as an elder.

b. The local church is figuratively referred to as a flock. What dangers to the people and elders exist if this image is pressed to an extreme, as some Christian groups have done?

8. a. What do you think Peter means when he says an elder should oversee the flock of God "voluntarily, according to the will of God"?

b. Evaluate the state of your own heart. Do you serve voluntarily, according to God's will?

9. a. Explain what the term *eagerness* means and how it makes an elder effective in his work.

b. Evaluate the state of your own heart. Do you eagerly oversee the Lord's household?

c. If you answer the above two questions in the negative, what do you think you should do?

10. The old saying, "Religion and money don't mix," bears some truth that is worth heeding. There is an exceptionally subtle temptation to serve God for money. Although no one—especially the one involved—would admit such a motive, it is quite common.

Many subconsciously think of church work as an easy, fulfilling job with pay. Others who are less subtle are consumed with gaining personal wealth and advantage. They see people and ministry in terms of dollar signs and always have a gimmick to seduce people and take their money. So do not be naive about the power money has over people's motives. As an elder, you must be very wise in distributing the church's money and choosing the people you give to.

a. Explain how the love of money destroyed the people described in the following verses: Judges 8:22-27; 16:4,5,18;

1 Samuel 2:29; 8:3; 2 Kings 5:15-27; John 12:3-6; Acts 5:1-10.

b. In specific terms, explain how the following servants of God illustrate questions eight, nine, and ten:

(1) Paul, Acts 20:33-35.

(2) Nehemiah, Neh. 5:14-19.

(3) Samuel, 1 Samuel 12:1-5.

(4) Moses, Numbers 16:15.

11.a. Why is an authoritarian display of oversight (B.E. page 24) in the family of God so sternly prohibited by Christ and His apostles (Matthew 18:4; 20:20-28; 1 Peter 1:22; 2:16; 3:8-11; 4:8; 5:5,6)?

b. What kind of damage would be done to a Christian community if the leaders ruled in a lordly, authoritarian manner? Consider 3 John 9-11, also B.E. pages 23-26.

Practical Exhortation:

In 1 Peter 5:3, Peter uses the phrase "those allotted to your charge." This seems to imply that a God-given number of people are allotted to the care of each eldership. Of course there are times of increase and decrease, but a specific number of people will generally remain constant over the years. This observation is not meant to give an assembly of believers an excuse to not evangelize or grow, but it is intended to encourage those who shepherd a small flock. I have been deeply moved by what Francis Schaeffer says about the prevalent obsession with "largeness" in his book, *No Little People:*

> As there are no little people in God's sight, so there are no little places. To be wholly committed to God in the place where God wants him — this is the creature glorified. . . . Nowhere more than in America are Christians caught in the twentieth-century syndrome of size. Size will show success. If I am

---

consecrated, there will necessarily be large quantities of people, dollars, etc. This is not so. Not only does God not say that size and spiritual power go together, but he even reverses this (especially in the teaching of Jesus) and tells us to be deliberately careful not to choose a place too big for us. We all tend to emphasize big works and big places, but all such emphasis is of the flesh. To think in such terms is simply to hearken back to the old, unconverted, egoist, self-centered *Me*. This attitude, taken from the world, is more dangerous to the Christian than fleshly amusement or practice. It is the flesh (*No Little People,* Downers Grove: InterVarsity Press, 1974, page 18).

12. a. Are you as a church leader aware of the power of your example for good and ill? The individual and corporate example of the elders as Christian men determines the quality of spiritual life in the church. Read carefully B.E. pages 80,81 and 26,27, then read together the following verses that show the importance of modeling Christ to others: 1 Corinthians 11:1; Philippians 3:17; 1 Thessalonians 1:6; 2 Thessalonians 3:6-10; Titus 2:7,8.

b. In 1 Timothy 4:12, the apostle writes to Timothy, "Let no one look down on your youthfulness, but rather in speech, conduct, love, faith and purity, show yourself an example of those who believe." Paul instructs Timothy to be a model in five spheres of life so that he may win the respect of the brethren. List these five spheres in order of your strongest area of exemplary living to your weakest.

c. Does Peter's emphasis on example mean that elders are to be passive leaders who merely display an exemplary life? What does Art Glasser mean when he says, "Passivity is an enemy" (B.E. page 29)?

106

13. Why is it of paramount importance to the saints that the elders be men who are "under authority"? Think about this question; it is a critical concept for both the elders and congregation.

14. a. The relationship between elders and congregation is supremely important. Evaluate your relationship with the congregation by marking the two statements below that best represent your situation.

(1) Strong, diligent leadership that always involves the congregation on important issues.

(2) Strong, diligent leadership that seldom involves the congregation on important issues.

(3) A committee that generally reflects the congregation's desires and goals.

(4) A leadership body that is paralyzed by fear of the congregation's opinions and wrath.

(5) An authoritarian leadership body that leaves the congregation in fear and infancy.

(6) A congregation that has confidence in its eldership.

(7) A congregation that is frustrated with its eldership.

(8) A congregation that has mixed feelings about its eldership.

(9) An assembly in which everyone agrees there is need for much improvement in the relationship between congregation and leadership.

b. Where do you as elders need to initiate improvements and changes in your relationship with the congregation? Be specific. (Read carefully B.E. page 30.)

SESSION TWELVE

FIRST PETER 5:4,5; HEBREWS 13:17 (B.E. pages 306-317)

Begin Your Session by Reading These Passages:

And when the Chief Shepherd appears, you will receive the unfading crown of glory. You younger men, likewise, be subject to your elders; and all of you, clothe yourselves with humility toward one another, for God is opposed to the proud, but gives grace to the humble. Humble yourselves, therefore, under the mighty hand of God, that He may exalt you at the proper time.

1 PETER 5:4-6

Obey your leaders, and submit to them; for they keep watch over your souls, as those who will give an account. Let them do this with joy and not with grief, for this would be unprofitable for you.

HEBREWS 13:17

Scripture Memory Assignment:
Hebrews 13:17.

1. a. What is the promised appearance of the Chief Shepherd meant to do for elders who face persecution, discouragement, or weariness?

b. I know of elders who are imprisoned and others who have lost their jobs solely because of their faith in Christ. These brethren live under constant oppression, suffer poverty, have little in the way of Christian literature, are hated and treated with contempt by the authorities, and have dim prospects for a better earthly life. What is unique about these elders is that they love to talk about the appearance of the Chief Shepherd. His appearance is constantly on their minds and in their speech, encouraging and motivating them.

We who live in free, prosperous countries tend to ignore the Chief Shepherd's return and our future glory. Because of our disinterest in His appearance and the rewards for faithful service, we are more likely to render half-hearted service—and even worse—to give up our work because of discouragement and conflicts. We urgently need to renew our minds and attitudes with the truth of the Chief Shepherd's appearance and His eternal rewards for elders who serve faithfully.

Evaluate how your awareness of the Chief Shepherd's return and His reward for faithful service affect your ministry. Choose three statements below that best represent your feelings. List them in order of their predominance in your thinking.

(1) I believe the doctrine, but it has little effect on my attitude or speech.

(2) I rarely think about it.

(3) I have no idea what it means.

(4) I long for His return, but that does not affect the quality of my work as an elder.

(5) I often think of His evaluation of my work upon His return, and that motivates me to greater service.

(6) I am encouraged and comforted by the thought

110

of His appearance; it keeps me going in the face of discouragement and setbacks.

(7) My work as an elder is unaffected by the thought of future reward.

c. Read these passages of Scripture about future reward to initiate your thinking and praying about the subject. Proverbs 27:18; John 12:26; Luke 19:12-26; 1 Corinthians 3:8,12-15; 4:5; 2 Corinthians 4:17; 5:10.

2. A good, Christian eldership, in God's eyes, is marked by humility. (Read B.E. page 31, paragraphs 2 and 3.) Yet too many elderships are characterized by pride. Thus they are easily deceived, quickly threatened by criticism and advice, hard to work with, stubborn, self-justifying, and displeasing to God. As Christ-like leaders, elders must clothe themselves in the garments of humility. Like our blessed Lord, elders must take up the servant's towel and wipe the feet of the saints (John 13:4,5). This is why Peter said to young men, elders, and all members, "You younger men, likewise, be subject to your elders; and all of you, clothe yourselves with humility toward one another" (1 Peter 5:5). Peter also writes, "To sum up, let all be harmonious, sympathetic, brotherly, kindhearted, and humble in spirit" (1 Peter 3:8).

Because humility is central to the spirit of the Christian community, look up the following verses and in one or two sentences summarize what you learn about humility or pride as they pertain to you as an elder. Obadiah 3; 2 Chronicles 26:3,4,16-21; 32:24-26; Proverbs 11:2(b); 6:16,17(a); 8:13; 13:10; 16:5,18; 18:12; 26:12; 29:23; Isaiah 66:2; Matthew 18:4; Romans 12:3; Galatians 5:26; Ephesians 4:1-3; Philippians 2:3-5; Colossians 3:12-14; 1 Peter 3:8. Discuss the truths you discovered from these texts that particularly touched your heart.

111

Without humility, leaders are likely to be threatened or become jealous of the younger men of the congregation. I have seen churches die because the elders were threatened by the younger men of the congregation; eventually, promising younger families left because they were psychologically forced out. If you as a body of elders are not developing the next generation of leaders and workers, you are slowly nailing the doors of your church closed forever.

As elders, you need to have an eye for the younger men of the church. You need to talk to them about their goals and values in life, encourage them in the Lord, direct them into responsible positions, and work with them. *Most elderships are too passive about this vital matter.* To counteract this problem, our church has developed an elder exposure program that has helped to actively encourage and challenge young men to eldership. (An outline of this program is found in Appendix C.) Look over the program and discuss if it would work for you.

3. a. Identify four traits that spiritually active, younger, adult men exhibit that commonly frighten church elders.

b. How can you as elders remove some of these common barriers without projecting a condescending attitude?

4. a. Note that in Hebrews the leaders watch over the "souls" of the Lord's people, which means their spiritual lives. Because watching over people's souls is more arduous and demanding than overseeing programs and institutions, few churches provide genuine, spiritual care for people. (See B.E. page 108,109). An increasing number of church leaders are simply administrators, organizers, promotion men, or public speakers. The spiritual lives of people are not their chief concern unless people come for counsel. That is one reason why there is little church discipline.

In specific terms, what is involved in watching over the souls of the Lord's people? (The book of Hebrews is an example of this. You should also read Matthew 18:12-14.)

Practical Suggestions:

Once a month, our elders go over a list of all the saints under our care to see if any have been missing or need help. We then assign visits and phone calls to each other. The following week we report on our assignments. I personally have found it helpful to go through my congregational directory weekly, to remind myself of who needs to be called, visited, or prayed for.

---

b. List some reasons why Christians need to belong to a local church where properly functioning elders watch over their spiritual welfare.

c. List some reasons why many people today are opposed to the idea of church elders watching over their spiritual welfare.

d. In which specific areas is it right for the church shepherds to involve themselves in the personal lives of the Lord's people? (Read B.E. pages 123-125.)

e. In which areas of believers' lives should the elders not extend their counsel and influence unless asked? (Read B.E. page 361.)

5. How does the teaching that you as an elder must render an account of your stewardship to the Lord affect your thinking and work?

6. a. What aspect of your work as an elder brings the greatest joy to your heart?

    b. What most grieves your heart as you shepherd the Lord's people?

Practical Warning:

    The emotional stresses and heavy burdens of caring for the spiritual welfare of people can break a man's health and his resolve to do the work. It is not the hard work or long hours that defeat a man; it is the emotional and spiritual stresses that crush a man's spirit. Specifically, constant fighting among believers, complaints, unbelief, and disobedience ultimately wear down a Christian elder. This is one reason why so few older men serve as elders.

    I have listed four thoughts to consider regarding your physical and spiritual welfare as an elder:

    (1) Remember that it is a privilege to suffer ill health for Jesus Christ (Philippians 1:29). Most people suffer broken health because of their sin or pursuit of earthly gain, but to suffer for the One Who endured untold suffering for us is a great honor.

    (2) At times it is appropriate to step aside, rest, and let other elders take the lead. When geese fly in their "V" formation, one takes the lead in order to break the wind and direct the others. As the lead bird tires, he drops to the outside and another assumes the lead position. This is how an eldership should work. If you are weary from taking the lead in resolving numerous problems and issues that confront the church, then step aside and let others move into the lead position. When you are rested and renewed, you can again move into the lead position.

    (3) In order to persevere in the battle, we all

---

need to learn to draw greater strength from the Lord. Alone we do not have the spiritual strength to endure fierce conflict with the rulers of darkness (Ephesians 6:10-17). But through prayer, faith, and the Word of God, we can appropriate His strength for our labors for Him (1 Samuel 30:6; Psalm 18:39; 86:16; Nehemiah 6:9; 8:10; Ezra 7:28; Isaiah 40:29,31; John 15:5; Ephesians 6:10; 2 Thessalonians 3:3; 2 Timothy 2:1; 4:17; 1 Peter 4:11; 5:10).

(4) Unrealistic or glorified ideas of Christian ministry eventually lead to disillusionment and discouragement. If there is any chance that you are naive about the shepherding ministry, the following verses will educate you to the harsh realities of working with people. Even Moses was broken by the people's incessant complaining and unbelief (Numbers 11:15).

(5) It would be a profitable exercise if you listed the major problems elders can expect to face when leading people. The following verses will help you on this optional assignment. Exodus 5:20,21; 16:22-30; 14:10-12; 15:23,24; 16:2-8; 17:1-7; Numbers 11:1-15; 12:1-3; 14:1-11,39-45; 16:1-14,41; 20:2-13; 21:4-9; 1 Samuel 8:19,20; 30:6; 2 Samuel 17:1-4; 19:40-20:2; 2 Chronicles 24:19; 33:10; 36:15,16.

7. a. An active, busy eldership needs lots of help, which is to be provided by the deacons. List specific responsibilities that you need relief from in order to give more time to caring for the people's spiritual welfare.

b. List specific ways you can better communicate with, guide, organize, and improve your accountability with the deacons. Remember, they need your input and guidance!

115

> **Practical Suggestions:**
> We have found that it is best for the moderator of the deacons to meet regularly with the elders so he can provide good communication between both groups. We have also had one of the elders meet regularly with the deacons. There are a number of options available that will facilitate good communication between the two groups, so use whatever suits your situation best.

8. For the final question read Luke 17:7-10. Explain what the parable means, especially to church elders.

APPENDIX (A)

One of the most essential ingredients of any kind of team-work is good communications. As a group of pastors coordinates its efforts, most of the problems which develop are the result of some common communication snags:

After the team has decided to do a certain thing, no one is actually assigned to do it. Everyone wonders why it doesn't get done . . .

In the areas of their group duties, each of the elders assumes that all the other men will take responsibility. So maybe no one ends up calling on Mrs. Eagleton in the hospital . . .

When a problem comes up in one of the areas of assigned responsibility, someone comes to complain to an elder who does not directly oversee that area. He tries to give solutions, but they don't coincide with what is really being planned in that area . . .

One of the elders sees something going wrong in an area that is normally supervised by another elder and steps in to provide counsel and advice to the workers. Having already been asked to do something different by the other elder, they are confused about whose directions they should follow . . .

One of the elders with keen interest in the study and presentation of the Word neglects his oversight of certain areas. As problems mount up in those areas, the other elders feel awkward about holding this hard working man responsible to fulfill his other duties and so nothing is said . . .

The following principles might help to head off such difficulties before they develop in a team setting:

A. Each pastor should set a goal for himself as a team member: "to rule well" or "to manage his responsibilities with skill and faithfulness" (1 Tim. 5:17).

Each pastor must visualize himself not just as a *minister* (teaching, preaching, counseling, praying, etc.) but as a *manager* (working with others, overseeing the work of others, developing and enforcing policies, planning for the future and evaluating progress etc.). Most pastors identify more with the *feeding* part of their task than with the *leading* part. This is particularly true for those without the gift of leading. By office, however, the elder's role is administrative ("overseer" = manager). Each of the elders could minister just fine *before* becoming an elder; what is added to his church functions as he becomes an elder is the responsibility of management or oversight. In order to underline the importance of this part of our duties, the pastors of our church have studied together through Olan Hendrix' *Management for the Christian Worker* (Santa Barbara: Quill Publications, 1976).

B. It is essential that each elder have a firm understanding of what he is responsible for.

In crass terms, this is called a "job description." He must know what his basic job is, his particular duties (so he doesn't neglect his job or try to do someone else's), whom he must report to for the fulfillment of his duties and who reports to him for the fulfillment of their duties.

This should be in writing and reviewed at least yearly (perhaps at an elders' retreat).

C. The regular meetings of the pastors should be well-planned and efficiently run.

Elders must meet together at least weekly to coordinate their supervision of church life. Their primary focus when gathered should be assessing the spiritual needs within the church family and praying with united hearts for God's moving in power to meet those needs and glorify Himself. Little time will be available for this prime function, however, if the business concerns of the council take up two hours every week. The answer? An efficiently planned and run business segment! Factors to be kept in mind include:

A prepared agenda in the hand of each elder. (We use a standardized sheet each week and fill in the agenda for that meeting. The chairman is responsible for the agenda and gives it at the beginning of each meeting.)

A place for each elder to record his personal tasks that are assigned during the meeting. (The agenda form has room for this. This removes any excuse for forgetfulness and causes us to define carefully what we are really supposed to do as we write it down.)

Careful chairmanship to insure that things move along smoothly without detours.

Review of delegated tasks and major decisions in order to "fix responsibility for follow-through" and give target dates for the accomplishment of tasks.

D. Each "worker" in the church answers only to one

person directly for his tasks.

For example, if Miss Harvey is a coordinator for several children's teachers in the Sunday learning center, she does not report haphazardly to any elder who might happen to check in on her. Rather she is assigned a line of reporting through one elder only (let's say Elder M has responsibility to oversee the teaching of children). If any other pastor has questions about the children's program under Miss Harvey, he doesn't quiz her. He goes straight to Elder M who in turn may need to communicate with Miss Harvey. (In similar fashion, the children's teachers who teach under Miss Harvey report directly to her only and receive their instructions from her only.) Elder M, on the other hand, answers to all his co-pastors for his oversight of the children's teaching. He must be open to their counsel, evaluations and corrections. (He can delegate the work to other people like Miss Harvey, but he cannot delegate his accountability to them. A supervisor is always responsible for the actions of his subordinates.) Together, the elders submit to the directions and evaluations of Christ.

E. A church calendar must be maintained for the sake of smooth planning.

When a church has a master calendar, conflicts are avoided and signals are not crossed. In a singular pastorate, many conflicts are avoided just because one person pretty well has his hand into everything and can inform others when a conflict of dates has arisen. The single pastor sometimes ends up as a portable "master calendar" and nothing gets planned without his approval or notification. Without such a singular "clearing house," a team of pastors needs to commit to the hand of the chairman or secretary of the council the responsibility for keeping a church calendar. This allows for the proper announcing of events in advance, etc. As a church grows larger and more active, this becomes more and more important.

F. The duties of particular elders should be made public knowledge within the congregation.

People in the church need to know which pastor to contact for different questions or comments they might have. Then, when a person has a question, for instance, about a coming retreat, he can contact the pastor who is responsible instead of wasting his time calling any other elders. All pastors must come to an understanding that they will handle only routine inquiries into areas they are not personally assigned to oversee. When a real problem comes up, they will direct the questioner to the appropriate elder. (Naturally, any pastor should have the responsibility to answer questions that pertain to the general oversight of the church and its goals.)

Though there are dozens of other management concepts which will help a group of elders work together harmoniously with one another and with others in the church, these six that we have presented are some of the "biggies" that must be seen in a team ministry if it is to survive very long as an effective and productive tool for edification. It is of greatest importance that the elders be humble men of prayer, who look daily to Christ for the direction of the church. As these men become unitedly aware of the goals Christ has for them, they will be able to manage with those high objectives in constant view, without getting sidetracked by the "little stuff" that frequently bogs church boards down for years on end. (*The Team Concept,* Tacoma: Hegg Bros. Printing, 1982, pages 177-181).

APPENDIX (B)

SAMPLE CHART

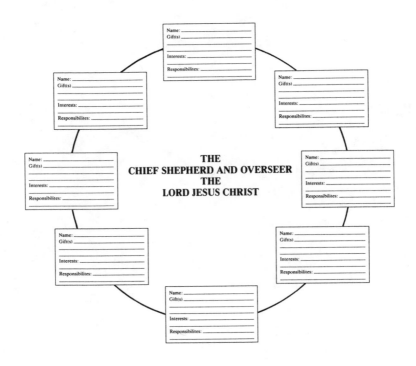

APPENDIX (C)
ELDER EXPOSURE PROGRAM

Purposes:
1. To expose all men in the congregation to the functions, procedures, work, and burdens of the oversight of God's household, even if they have no plans or desire to be elders. Note: This program does not qualify or automatically make one an elder.
2. To give exposure and training in the work of caring for God's people to prospective missionaries, elders, and deacons.
3. To inspire more men to assume the responsibility of caring for God's household.

Procedures:
1. The elders select one or two men from the congregation to meet with the present elders for a period of four to six months.
2. The men selected are expected to attend all the elders' meetings. They would fully participate in all discussions, but decision making would be limited to the elders.
3. The men selected would consistently attend all regular church meetings.
4. The men selected would be available to accompany elders on some visits.

5. The men selected would keep all personal and private matters confidential. If a discussion is one of a highly delicate and personal nature, the observer would be asked to excuse himself.